ADVENTURE AWAITS

>> by Knit Picks

Copyright 2019 © Knit Picks

All rights reserved. This book or any portion thereof may not be reproduced or used in any manner whatsoever without the express written permission of the publisher except for the use of brief quotations in a book review.

Photography by John Cranford

Printed in the United States of America

First Printing, 2019

ISBN 978-1-62767-223-8

Versa Press, Inc.

800-447-7829

www.versapress.com

CONTENTS

5 Point Bomber	7
Alastair Vest	17
Bargeman	23
Eye of Partridge Hiking Socks	27
Hurricane Ridge Pullover	31
Kai Hat, Cowl, and Long Scarf	37
Ogee Hat and Scarf	43
Oriel	49
Slade Pullover	59
Snug Gloves	65
Syncopated Brioche Cowl	69
Timberline Mittens	75
Trailhead Socks	79
Valen	83
Wayfarer Vest	89
Wembley Sweater	95

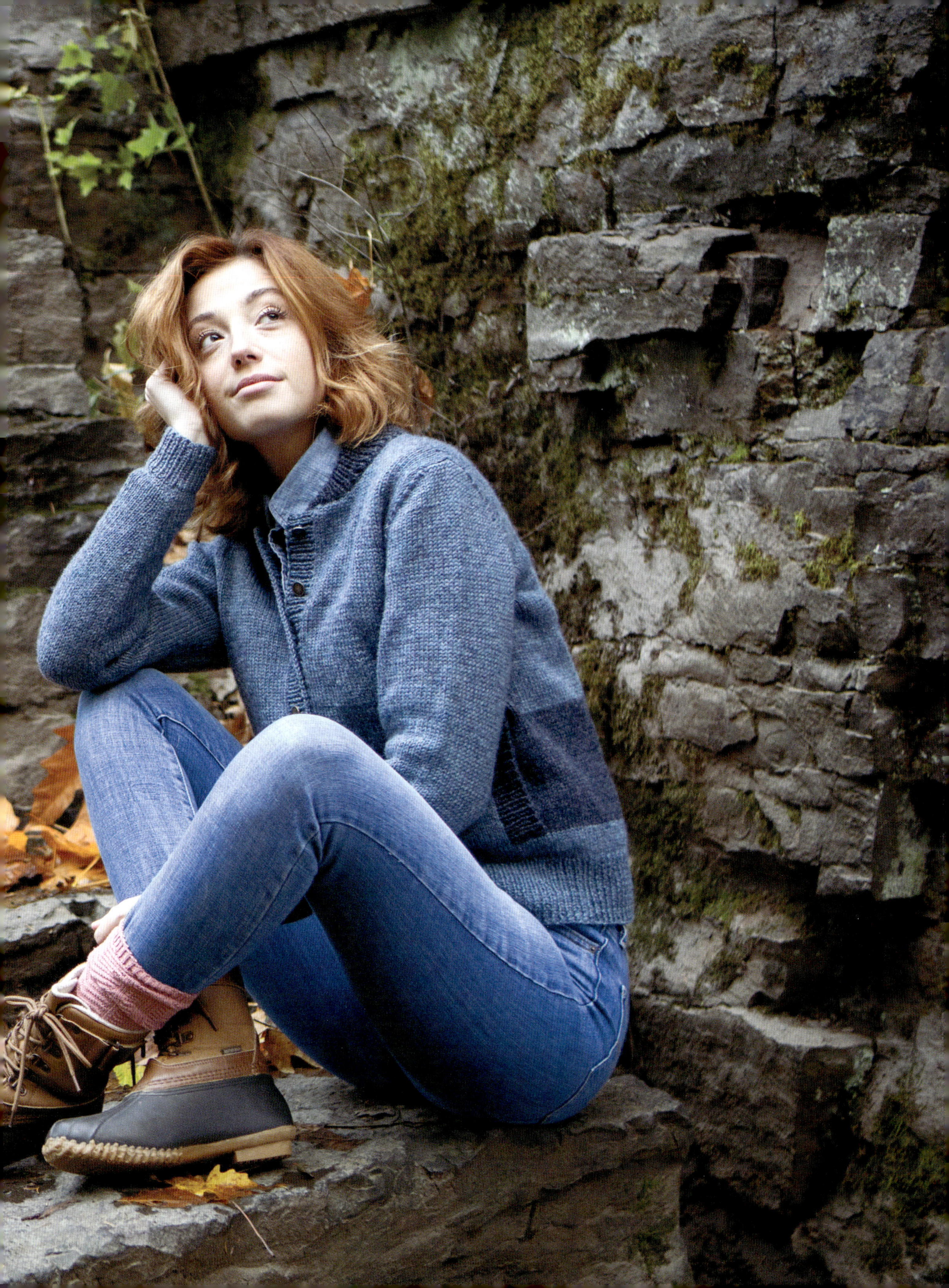

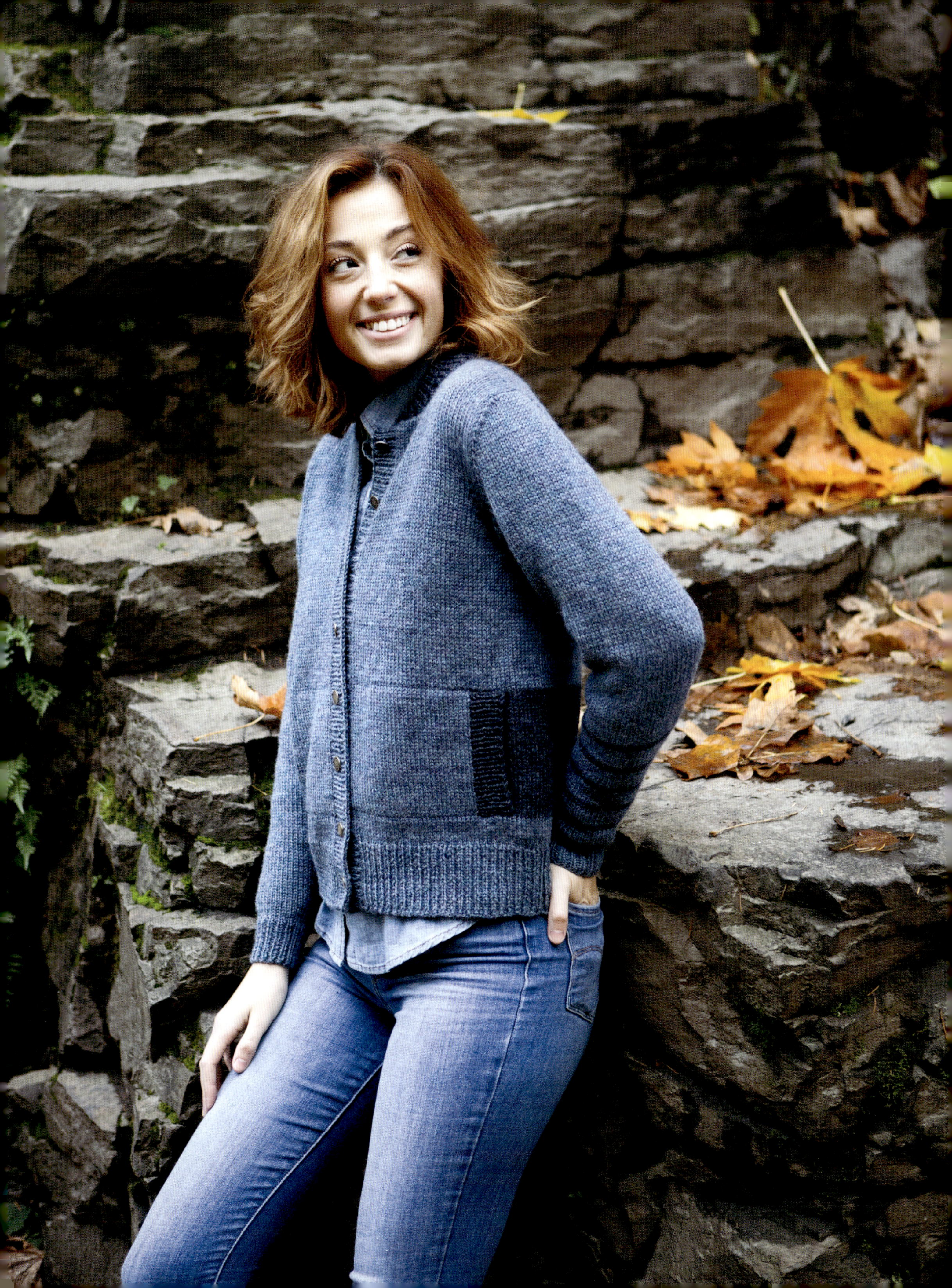

5 POINT BOMBER

by Holli Yeoh

FINISHED MEASUREMENTS
36 (38.25, 41, 45.25, 48.5, 53.25, 57.5, 60.75, 65, 68.75)" finished bust measurement; garment is meant to be worn with 3.5 to 4.5" of ease

YARN
Knit Picks Wool of the Andes (worsted weight, 100% Peruvian Highland Wool; 110 yards/50g): MC Icicle Heather 25992, 10 (11, 12, 13, 14, 15, 17, 18, 19, 19) skeins, C1 Onyx Heather 24076, 3 (3, 3, 3, 4, 4, 4, 4, 4, 4) skeins

NEEDLES
US 5 (3.75mm) straight or circular needles, or size to obtain gauge

US 3 (3.25mm) straight or circular needles, or size two sizes smaller than needles to obtain gauge

NOTIONS
Yarn Needle
Stitch Markers, including 1 Locking
Scrap Yarn or Stitch Holder
8 (8, 8, 8, 8, 8, 9, 9, 9, 9) 1" Buttons

GAUGE
21 sts and 29 rows = 4" in stockinette stitch, blocked

For pattern support, contact info@holliyeoh.com

5 Point Bomber

Notes:

Bold color blocking and narrow stripes, inspired by Canada's iconic Hudson Bay Company blankets, bring new energy to the classic bomber jacket. The wide contrast waist slides perfectly into a kangaroo pouch pocket, adding a flattering visual effect.

The bottom-up, seamed construction ensures a great fit and structure, with the traditional high collar to keep you cozy on blustery days,

Short rows are used to shape both the shoulders and the collar. Because the German Short Row method is recommended for the collar, all the short row instructions are written for this method. Feel free to use your preferred method.

German Short Rows

I favor this method when working short rows across a stitch pattern with knits and purls appearing on the same side, such as ribbing. There is no need to fiddle with wrapping stitches and then hiding the wrap later.
Work to turning point; turn. WYIF, SL the first st P-wise. Bring yarn over the back of the right needle, pulling firmly to create a "double stitch" on the right needle. If the next st is a K st, leave the yarn at the back; if the next st is a P st, bring the yarn to the front between the needles. When it's time to work into the double st, knit both strands tog.

Stripe Sequence

Working in St st, work (2 rows C1, 6 rows MC) 4 times, 2 rows C1. When 34 rows of Stripe Sequence are completed, resume with MC.

German Short Row (GSR)

The turning point (or gap) just before the double st created by the German Short Row technique.

Right-Slanting Raised Increase (RRI)

With right needle, K into right shoulder of st in row directly below the next st on left needle. 1 st inc.

Left-Slanting Raised Increase (LRI)

Use left needle to pick up st 2 rows directly below last st worked and K into it. 1 st inc.

3-Needle Bind Off

A tutorial for the 3-Needle Bind Off can be found at https://tutorials.knitpicks.com/3-needle-bind-off/.

DIRECTIONS

Back

Ribbing

With smaller needle and MC, CO 92 (100, 106, 116, 124, 134, 146, 156, 166, 176) sts.
Row 1 (RS): K1, *K1, P1; rep from * to last st, K1.
Row 2 (WS): P1, *K1, P1; rep from * to last st, P1.
Rep last 2 rows 10 more times.

Body

Change to larger needles.
Inc Row (RS): K11 (11, 15, 13, 13, 11, 13, 13, 13, 11), RRI, *K24 (26, 26, 30, 20, 16, 24, 26, 28, 22), RRI; rep from * 2 (2, 2, 2, 4, 6, 4, 4, 4, 6) times more, K remaining 9 (11, 13, 13, 11, 11, 13, 13, 13, 11) sts. 96 (104, 110, 120, 130, 142, 152, 162, 172, 184) sts.
Beginning with a P row, work in St st until piece measures 4.5 (4.25, 4.25, 4.75, 4.75, 4.5, 4.5, 4.5, 4.5, 4)" from beginning, ending with a WS row. Break yarn.
With C1, work even in St st for 38 rows, ending with a WS row. Break yarn.
With MC, work even in St st until piece measures 14.75 (15, 15.25, 15.75, 15.75, 15.25, 15.5, 16, 16.25, 16)" from beginning, ending with a WS row.

Armhole Shaping

BO 5 (6, 8, 9, 11, 11, 12, 11, 12, 13) sts at beginning of next 2 rows. 86 (92, 94, 102, 108, 120, 128, 140, 148, 158) sts.

Sizes 57.5, 60.75, 65, 68.75" Only
Double Dec Row (RS): K2, K3tog, K to last 5 sts, SSSK, K2. 4 sts dec.
Rep Double Dec Row - (-, -, -, -, -, 0, 1, 1, 2) more time(s). 86 (92, 94, 102, 108, 120, 124, 132, 140, 146) sts.

All Sizes
Dec Row (RS): K2, K2tog, K to last 4 sts, SSK, K2. 2 sts dec.
Rep Dec Row every RS row 4 (6, 6, 8, 11, 15, 15, 17, 18, 18) more times. 76 (78, 80, 84, 84, 88, 92, 96, 102, 108) sts.
Work even in St st until armhole measures 6.5 (6.75, 6.75, 7, 7.25, 7.5, 7.75, 7.75, 8, 8.25)" from underarm BO, ending with a RS row.
Next Row (WS): P18 (19, 20, 21, 21, 23, 24, 26, 29, 32) sts, PM#1, P10, PM#2, P20 (20, 20, 22, 22, 22, 24, 24, 24, 24), PM#3, P10, PM#4, P to end. When viewing Ms from RS they are counted from left to right.

Shoulder and Neck Shaping

Both shoulders and neck are shaped with short rows throughout.
Short Rows 1 (RS) & 2 (WS): Work to last 4 (4, 4, 4, 4, 4, 5, 5, 6) sts, turn.
Short Rows 3 & 4: Work to 4 (4, 4, 4, 4, 4, 5, 5, 6) sts before last GSR, turn.

Sizes 41, 45.25, 48.5, 53.25, 57.5, 60.75, 65, 68.75" Only
Short Rows 5 & 6: Work to - (-, 3, 4, 4, 4, 4, 5, 5) sts before last GSR, turn.

All Sizes
Short Row 7: Work to 3 (4, 3, 3, 3, 4, 4, 4, 5) sts before last GSR, turn.
Short Row 8: Work to M#2, turn.
Short Row 9: Work to 3 (3, 3, 3, 3, 3, 4, 4, 4, 5) sts beyond M#1, turn.
Short Row 10: Work 3 (3, 3, 3, 3, 4, 4, 4, 5) sts, turn.
Short Row 11 (RS): Work to end.

Short Row 12: Work to 6 (7, 6, 6, 7, 8, 8, 9, 10) sts beyond M#4, turn.
Short Row 13: Work to M#3, turn.
Short Row 14: Work to 3 (3, 3, 3, 3, 4, 4, 4, 5) sts beyond M#4, turn.
Short Row 15: Work 3 (3, 3, 3, 3, 4, 4, 4, 5) sts, turn.
Short Row 16: Work to end.
Row 17 (RS): Work to M#4, BO all sts to M#1, work to end. 18 (19, 20, 21, 21, 23, 24, 26, 29, 32) sts each shoulder. Transfer sts to holders.

Left Front

Ribbing
With smaller needle and MC, CO 44 (46, 50, 54, 58, 64, 70, 74, 80, 86) sts.
Row 1 (RS): K1, *K1, P1; rep from * to last st, K1.
Row 2 (WS): P1, *K1, P1; rep from * to last st, P1.
Rep last 2 rows 10 more times.

Body
Change to larger needle.
Inc Row (RS): K11 (11, 13, 7, 9, 9, 11, 11, 21), RRI, *K22 (24, 26, 14, 14, 16, 18, 18, 20, 44), RRI; rep from * 0 (0, 0, 2, 2, 2, 2, 2, 2, 0) more times, K remaining 11 (11, 11, 5, 7, 7, 7, 9, 9, 21) sts. 46 (48, 52, 58, 62, 68, 74, 78, 84, 88) sts.
Beginning with a P row, work in St st until piece measures 4.5 (4.25, 4.25, 4.75, 4.75, 4.5, 4.5, 4.5, 4.5, 4)" from beginning, ending with a WS row. Break yarn.
Next Row (RS): With C1, K15 (15, 17, 23, 24, 30, 36, 40, 46, 50), place locking M between sts in row below, K to end. Work even in St st for 37 rows more. Break yarn. Place sts on a holder.

Pocket Front
Using larger needle and MC, with RS facing, PU and K into right leg of MC sts in last row before color change between M and left edge. 31 (33, 35, 35, 38, 38, 38, 38, 38, 38) sts. Work even in St st for 37 more rows. Break yarn.

Join Pocket Top
Transfer held sts to a spare needle (it can be smaller). Join pocket by holding MC pocket sts in front of C1 body sts, with MC, K15 (15, 17, 23, 24, 30, 36, 40, 46, 50), *insert right needle into next st on both front needle and back needle and K those 2 sts tog; rep from * to end of row.
Work even in St st until piece measures 14.75 (15, 15.25, 15.75, 15.75, 15.25, 15.5, 16, 16.25, 16)" from beginning, ending with a WS row.

Armhole Shaping
BO 5 (6, 8, 9, 11, 11, 12, 11, 12, 13) sts at beginning of next row. 41 (42, 44, 49, 51, 57, 62, 67, 72, 75) sts.
Work 1 WS row.

Sizes 57.5, 60.75, 65, 68.75" Only
Double Dec Row (RS): K2, K3tog, K to end of row. 2 sts dec. Rep Double Dec Row – (–, –, –, –, –, 0, 1, 1, 2) more time(s). 41 (42, 44, 49, 51, 57, 60, 63, 68, 69) sts.

All Sizes
Dec Row (RS): K2, K2tog, K to end of row. 1 st dec.

Rep Dec Row every RS row 4 (6, 6, 8, 11, 15, 15, 17, 18, 18) times more. 36 (35, 37, 40, 39, 41, 44, 45, 49, 50) sts. Work even in St st until armhole measures 5.25 (5.25, 5.25, 5.5, 5.75, 6.25, 6.5, 6.5, 6.75, 7)" from underarm BO, ending with a RS row.

Neck Shaping

BO 8 (6, 7, 9, 8, 8, 10, 9, 10, 8) sts P-wise at beginning of next WS row. 28 (29, 30, 31, 31, 33, 34, 36, 39, 42) sts.
Work 1 RS row.
BO 3 sts P-wise at beginning of next WS row.
Work 1 RS row.
BO 2 sts P-wise at beginning of every WS row twice.
BO 1 st P-wise at beginning of every WS row 3 times. 18 (19, 20, 21, 21, 23, 24, 26, 29, 32) sts remain.
Work even in St st until armhole measures 6.75 (7, 7, 7.25, 7.5, 7.75, 8, 8, 8.25, 8.5)" from underarm BO, ending with a RS row.

Shoulder Shaping

Short Rows 1 (WS) & 2 (RS): Work to last 4 (4, 4, 4, 4, 4, 4, 5, 5, 6) sts, turn. Work to end.
Short Rows 3 & 4: Work to 4 (4, 4, 4, 4, 4, 4, 5, 5, 6) sts before last GSR, turn. Work to end.
Short Rows 5 & 6: Work to 4 (4, 3, 4, 4, 4, 4, 4, 5, 5) sts before last GSR, turn. Work to end.

Sizes 41, 45.25, 48.5, 53.25, 57.5, 60.75, 65, 68.75" Only

Short Rows 7 & 8: Work to – (–, 3, 3, 3, 4, 4, 4, 5) sts before last GSR, turn. Work to end.

All Sizes

Short Rows 9 & 10: Work 3 (3, 3, 3, 3, 4, 4, 4, 5) sts, turn. Work to end.
Next Row (WS): Purl all sts.
Place shoulder sts on a holder. Break yarn, leaving a tail approximately 26 (27, 28, 28, 28, 30, 31, 32, 35, 37)" long to be used later in a 3-Needle Bind Off.

Right Front

Work as for Left Front until piece measures 4.5 (4.25, 4.25, 4.75, 4.75, 4.5, 4.5, 4.5, 4.5, 4)" from beginning, ending with a WS row. Break yarn.
Next Row (RS): With C1, K31 (33, 35, 35, 38, 38, 38, 38, 38, 38) sts, place locking M between sts in row below, K to end. Work even in St st for 37 more rows. Break yarn. Place sts on a holder.

Pocket Front

Using larger needle and MC, with RS facing, PU and K into right leg of MC sts in last row before color change between right edge and M. 31 (33, 35, 35, 38, 38, 38, 38, 38, 38) sts. Work even in St st for 37 more rows. Break yarn.

Join Pocket Top

Transfer held sts to a spare needle (it can be smaller). Join pocket by holding MC pocket sts in front of C1 body sts, with MC, *insert right needle into next st on both front needle and back needle and K those 2 sts tog; rep from * for all pocket sts, K to end of row.

Work even in St st until piece measures 14.75 (15, 15.25, 15.75, 15.75, 15.25, 15.5, 16, 16.25, 16)" from beginning, ending with a RS row.

Armhole Shaping
BO 5 (6, 8, 9, 11, 11, 12, 11, 12, 13) sts at beginning of next row. 41 (42, 44, 49, 51, 57, 62, 67, 72, 75) sts.

Sizes 57.5, 60.75, 65, 68.75" Only
Double Dec Row (RS): K to last 5 sts, SSSK, K2. 2 sts dec.
Rep Double Dec Row – (–, –, –, –, –, 0, 1, 1, 2) more time(s). 41 (42, 44, 49, 51, 57, 60, 63, 68, 69) sts.

All Sizes
Dec Row (RS): K to last 4 sts, SSK, K2. 1 st dec.
Rep Dec Row every RS row 4 (6, 6, 8, 11, 15, 15, 17, 18, 18) more times. 36 (35, 37, 40, 39, 41, 44, 45, 49, 50) sts.
Work even in St st until armhole measures 5.25 (5.25, 5.25, 5.5, 5.75, 6.25, 6.5, 6.5, 6.75, 7)" from underarm BO, ending with a WS row.

Neck Shaping
BO 8 (6, 7, 9, 8, 8, 10, 9, 10, 8) sts at beginning of next RS row. 28 (29, 30, 31, 31, 33, 34, 36, 39, 42) sts.
Work 1 WS row.
BO 3 sts at beginning of next RS row.
Work 1 WS row.
BO 2 sts at beginning of every RS row twice.
BO 1 st at beginning of every RS row 3 times. 18 (19, 20, 21, 21, 23, 24, 26, 29, 32) sts remain.
Work even in St st until armhole measures 6.75 (7, 7, 7.25, 7.5, 7.75, 8, 8, 8.25, 8.5)" from underarm BO, ending with a WS row.

Shoulder Shaping
Short Rows 1 (RS) & 2 (WS): Work to last 4 (4, 4, 4, 4, 4, 4, 5, 5, 6) sts, turn. Work to end.
Short Rows 3 & 4: Work to 4 (4, 4, 4, 4, 4, 4, 5, 5, 6) sts before last GSR, turn. Work to end.
Short Rows 5 & 6: Work to 4 (4, 3, 4, 4, 4, 4, 4, 5, 5) sts before last GSR, turn. Work to end.

Sizes 41, 45.25, 48.5, 53.25, 57.5, 60.75, 65, 68.75" Only
Short Rows 7 & 8: Work to – (–, 3, 3, 3, 3, 4, 4, 4, 5) sts before last GSR, turn. Work to end.

All Sizes
Short Rows 9 & 10: Work 3 (3, 3, 3, 3, 3, 4, 4, 4, 5) sts, turn. Work to end.
Next Row (RS): Knit all sts.
Place shoulder sts on a holder. Break yarn, leaving a tail approximately 26 (27, 28, 28, 28, 30, 31, 32, 35, 37)" long.

Left Sleeve
Ribbing
With MC and smaller needles, CO 42 (42, 42, 42, 44, 46, 46, 48, 50, 50) sts.
Row 1 (RS): K1, *K1, P1; rep from * to last st, K1.
Row 2 (WS): P1, *K1, P1; rep from * to last st, P1.
Rep last 2 rows 7 more times.
Change to larger needles.

Beginning with a K row, work in St st until piece measures 3.25" from beginning, ending with a WS row.

Begin Stripe Sequence
Work first 2 rows of Stripe Sequence.

Sleeve Shaping
Cont Stripe Sequence throughout Sleeve Shaping (as follows); when last row of Stripe Sequence is complete, work in MC only.
Inc Row (RS): K2, RRI, K to last 2 sts, LRI, K2. 2 sts inc.
Working in St st, rep Inc Row every 6 (4, 4, 4, 4, 2, 2, 2, 2, 2) rows 8 (2, 6, 13, 22, 6, 11, 11, 11, 13) more times, then every 8 (6, 6, 6, –, 4, 4, 4, 4, 4) rows 4 (12, 10, 6, –, 18, 16, 16, 15, 13) time(s). 68 (72, 76, 82, 90, 96, 102, 104, 104, 104) sts.
Work even until sleeve measures 17.75 (18, 18.5, 19, 19, 18.75, 18.75, 18.75, 18.25, 17.5)" from beginning, ending with a WS row.

Sleeve Cap Shaping
BO 5 (6, 8, 9, 11, 11, 12, 11, 12, 13) sts at beginning of next 2 rows. 58 (60, 60, 64, 68, 74, 78, 82, 80, 78) sts.
Double Dec Row (RS): K2, K3tog, K to last 5 sts, SSSK, K2. 4 sts dec.

Rep Double Dec Row 3 (3, 3, 4, 5, 7, 7, 9, 6, 2) more time(s), ending with a WS row. 42 (44, 44, 44, 44, 42, 46, 42, 52, 66) sts.
Single Dec Row (RS): K2, K2tog, K to last 4 sts, SSK, K2. 2 sts dec.
Rep Single Dec Row 6 (7, 7, 7, 6, 5, 5, 3, 8, 15) more times, ending with a WS row. 28 (28, 28, 28, 30, 30, 34, 34, 34, 34) sts.
Rep Double Dec Row 3 times. 16 (16, 16, 16, 18, 18, 22, 22, 22, 22) sts.
BO all sts.

Right Sleeve

Work as for Left Sleeve, replacing Stripe Sequence with MC.

Finishing

Block to schematic measurements.

Button Band
With RS facing, smaller needles and MC, PU and K 105 (107, 109, 111, 111, 111, 119, 119, 121, 121) sts evenly along Left Front edge from neckline to CO edge.
Inc Row (WS): PFB, *K1, P1; rep from * to last 2 sts, K1, PFB. 107 (109, 111, 113, 113, 113, 121, 121, 123, 123) sts.
Begin 1x1 Rib
Row 1 (RS): K2, *K1, P1; rep from * to last st, K1.
Row 2 (WS): P2, *K1, P1; rep from * to last st, P1.
Work 6 more rows in ribbing as established, ending with a WS row.
BO loosely in pattern.

Buttonhole Band
With RS facing, smaller needles and MC, PU and K 105 (107, 109, 111, 111, 111, 119, 119, 121, 121) sts evenly spaced along Right Front from CO edge to neckline.
Inc Row (WS): PFB, *K1, P1; rep from * to last 2 sts, K1, PFB. 107 (109, 111, 113, 113, 113, 121, 121, 123, 123) sts.
Begin 1x1 Rib
Row 1 (RS): K2, *P1, K1; rep from * to last st, K1.
Row 2 (WS): P2, *K1, P1; rep from * to last st, P1.
Buttonhole Row 1 (RS): Work 3 (5, 7, 9, 9, 9, 3, 3, 5, 5) sts, *PM, K1, YO, K2tog, work 11 sts; rep from * to last 6 sts, PM, K1, YO, K2tog, work to end. 8 (8, 8, 8, 8, 8, 9, 9, 9, 9) buttonholes.
Buttonhole Row 2 (WS): *Work in pattern to 2 sts before M, drop YO from the previous row, P1, SM; rep from * to last 6 (8, 10, 12, 12, 12, 6, 6, 8, 8) sts, work to end of row.
Buttonhole Row 3: *Work in pattern to M, remove M, K1, P1 under the loose strand from the YO 2 rows below and the bar between sts from 1 row below; rep from * to last 4 sts, then work to end of row.
Work 3 more rows in ribbing as established, ending with a WS row.
BO loosely in pattern.

Pocket Edging (make 2 the same)
With RS facing, using C1 and smaller needles, PU and K 27 sts along pocket opening edge.
Inc Row (WS): PFB, *K1, P1; rep from * to last 2 sts, K1, PFB. 29 sts.
Begin 1x1 Rib
Row 1 (RS): K2, *P1, K1; rep from * to last st, K1.
Row 2 (WS): P2, *K1, P1; rep from * to last st, P1.
Work 5 more rows in ribbing as established, ending with a RS row.
BO loosely in pattern on WS.
Steam block edging, stretch it to length of pocket opening, pin and allow to dry. Sew down sides of edging to Front using Mattress st.

Join Shoulders
Right Shoulder: Holding RS tog and with long tail, join right shoulder seam using 3-Needle Bind Off, working from armhole to neck edge.
Left Shoulder: Work as for right shoulder but BO P-wise from armhole to neck edge.

Collar
Collar is shaped with short rows. For this design, I recommend using the German Short Row method.
With RS facing, smaller needles and C1, beginning and ending halfway across top of front bands, PU and K 27 (26, 29, 31, 30, 30, 32, 31, 32, 30) sts along Right Front neck to shoulder, 42 (42, 42, 44, 44, 44, 46, 46, 46, 46) sts along Back neck to left shoulder, then 27 (26, 29, 31, 30, 30, 32, 31, 32, 30) sts along Left Front neck. 96 (94, 100, 106, 104, 104, 110, 108, 110, 106) sts.
Setup Row (WS): P1, (P1, K1) 1 (1, 2, 4, 3, 3, 5, 4, 5, 4) time(s), *PFB, (P1, K1) 5 times; rep from * 7 more times, PFB, (P1, K1) 1 (0, 2, 3, 3, 3, 4, 4, 4, 3) time(s), P2. 105 (103, 109, 115, 113, 113, 119, 117, 119, 115) sts.
Short Row 1 (RS): Working in 1x1 Rib as established, work 24 sts, PM, work 52 (50, 56, 62, 60, 60, 62, 64, 66, 62) sts; turn, PM.
Short Row 2: Work to M, turn.
Short Row 3: Work to M, remove M, work 3 sts, PM, turn.
Short Rows 4 to 16: Rep Short Row 3 until all neckline sts have been worked, ending at Right Front edge.
Row 17 (RS): Work 1 row in pattern.
Row 18 (WS): Work 3 sts, PM, work in pattern to end.
Short Row 19: Work 3 sts (first st is German Short Row double stitch), PM, work to M, remove M, turn.
Short Rows 20 to 32: Rep Short Row 19. 52 (50, 56, 62, 60, 60, 62, 64, 66, 62) sts between Ms.
Work to end of row for next 2 rows.
Fold collar to inside and graft sts to picked up sts.

Seams
Steam block collar and front bands, stretching and pinning in place until dry. Sew in sleeves matching BO edges and center of sleeve top with the shoulder seam. Using Mattress st, sew sleeve and side seams. Weave in ends. Sew on buttons to correspond with buttonholes.

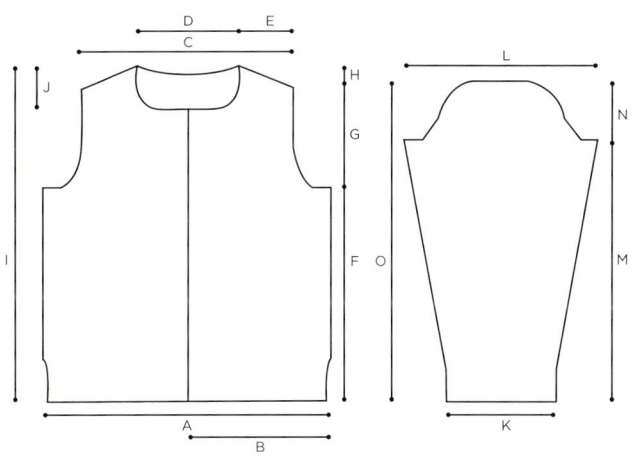

- **A:** 18.25 (19.75, 21, 22.75, 24.75, 27, 29, 30.75, 32.75, 35)"
- **B:** 8.75 (9.25, 10, 11, 11.75, 13, 14, 14.75, 16, 16.75)"
- **C:** 14.5 (14.75, 15.25, 16, 16, 16.75, 17.5, 18.25, 19.5, 20.5)"
- **D:** 7.5 (7.5, 7.5, 8, 8, 8, 8.5, 8.5, 8.5, 8.5)"
- **E:** 3.5 (3.5, 3.75, 4, 4, 4.5, 4.5, 5, 5.5, 6)"
- **F:** 14.75 (15, 15.25, 15.75, 15.75, 15.25, 15.5, 16, 16.25, 16)"
- **G:** 6.75 (7, 7, 7.25, 7.5, 7.75, 8, 8, 8.25, 8.5)"
- **H:** 1 (1, 1.5, 1.5, 1.5, 1.5, 1.5, 1.5, 1.5, 1.5)"
- **I:** 22.5 (23, 23.5, 24.25, 24.5, 25, 24.5, 25, 25.5, 26, 26)"
- **J:** 2.5 (2.75, 3, 3, 3, 3, 3, 3, 3, 3)"
- **K:** 8 (8, 8, 8, 8.5, 8.75, 8.75, 9.25, 9.5, 9.5)"
- **L:** 13 (13.75, 14.5, 15.5, 17.25, 18.25, 19.5, 19.75, 19.75, 19.75)"
- **M:** 17.75 (18, 18.5, 19, 19, 18.75, 18.75, 18.75, 18.25, 17.5)"
- **N:** 4.25 (4.5, 4.5, 4.75, 4.75, 5, 5, 5, 5.5, 6.25)"
- **O:** 22 (22.5, 23, 23.75, 23.75, 23.75, 23.75, 23.75, 23.75, 23.75)"

5 Point Bomber

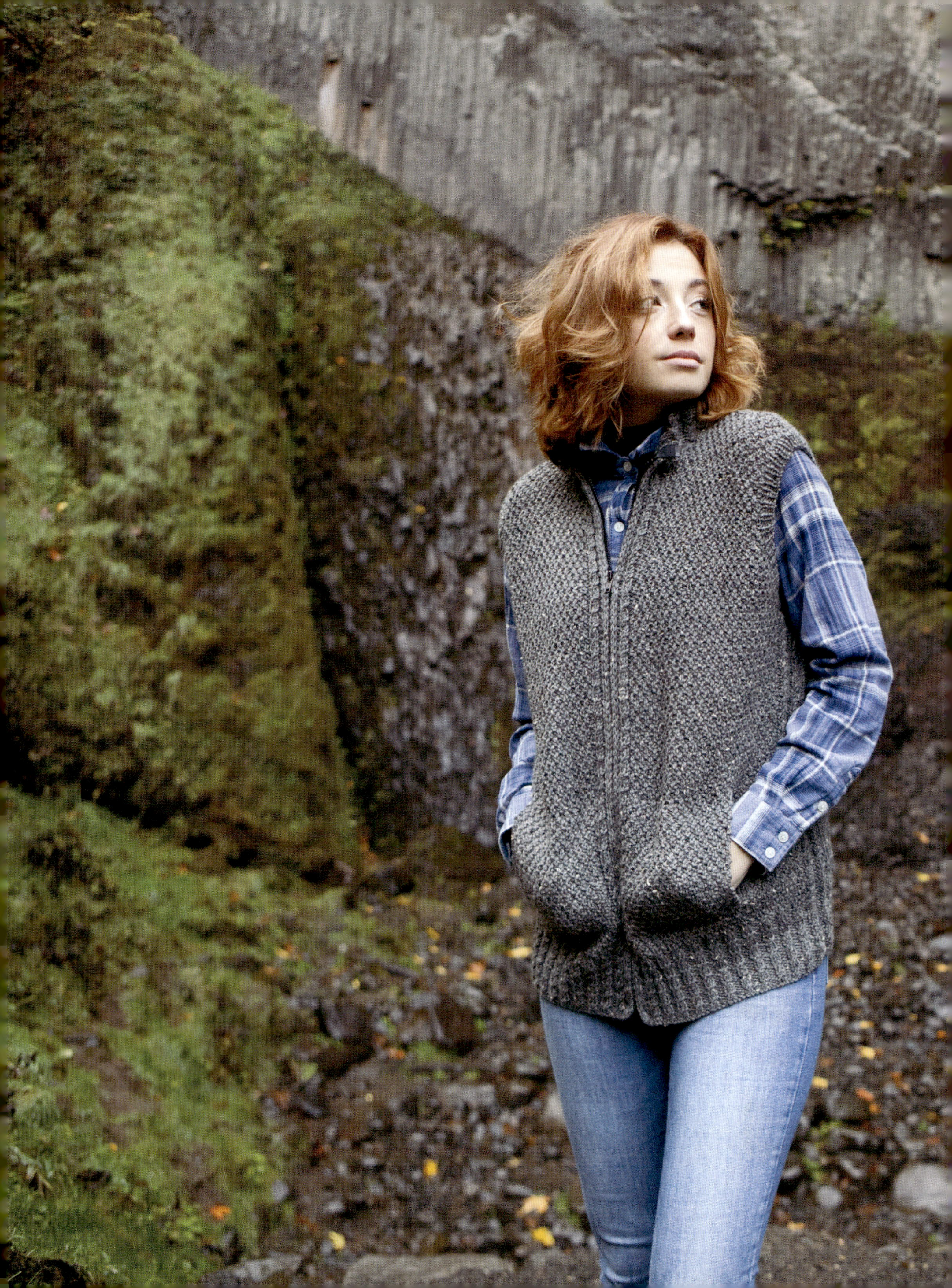

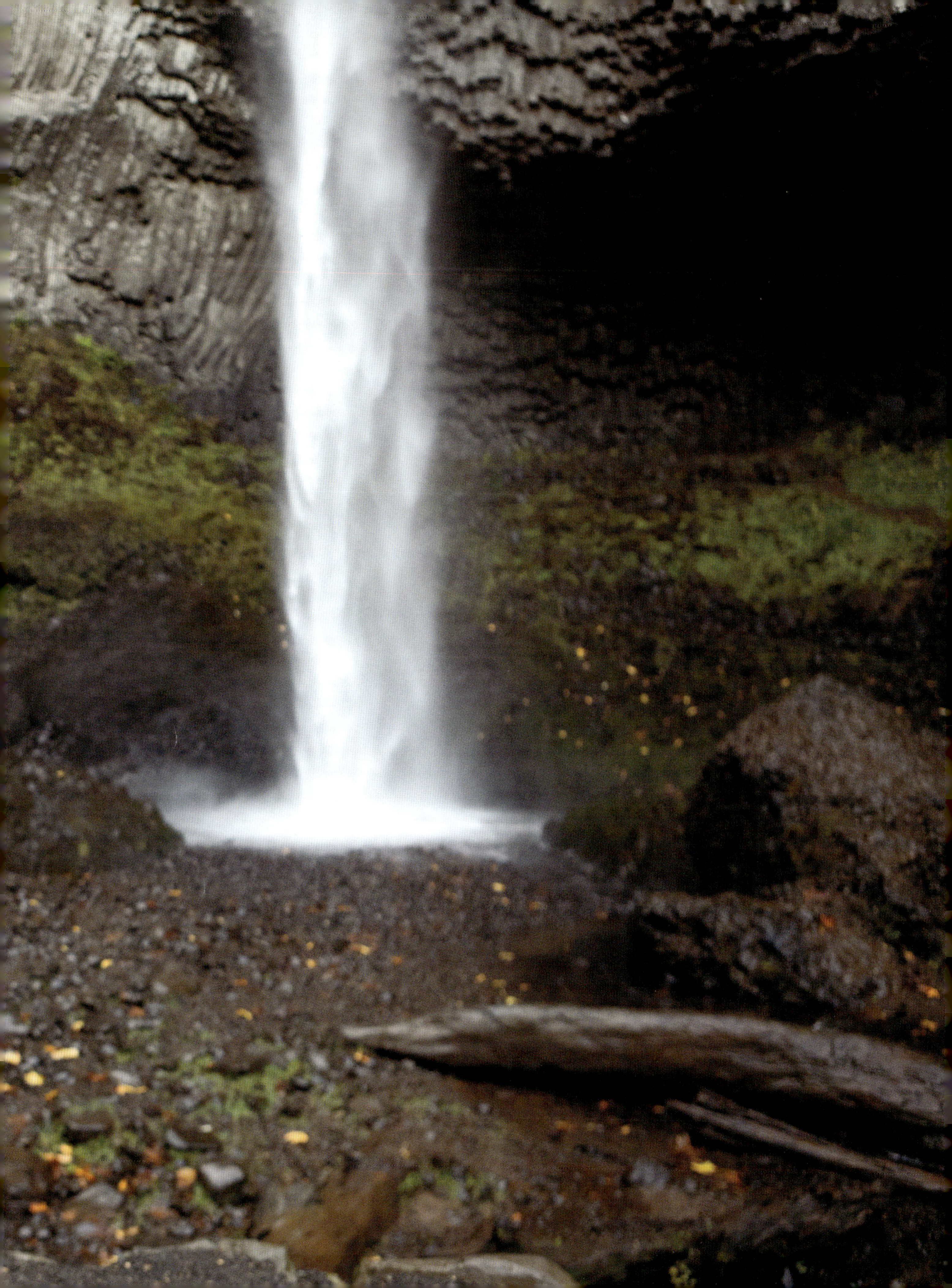

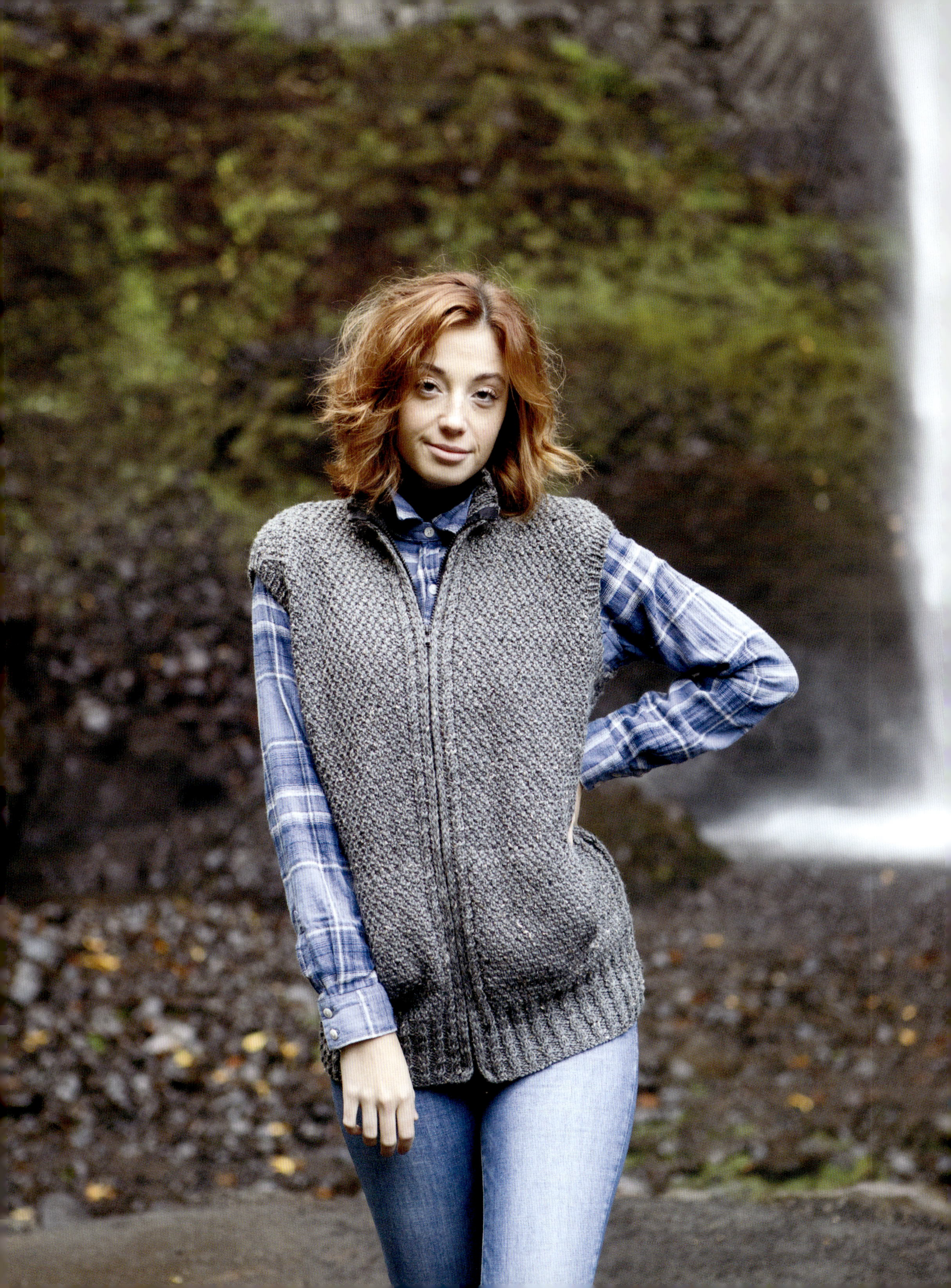

ALASTAIR VEST

by Frances Othen-Wales

FINISHED MEASUREMENTS
38 (41.25, 44.75, 48, 51.25, 54.75)" finished chest measurement; garment is meant to be worn with 2-4" of positive ease

YARN
Knit Picks Wool of the Andes Tweed (worsted weight, 80% Peruvian Highland Wool, 20% Donegal Tweed; 110 yards/50g): Flagstone Heather 25457, 8 (9, 10, 12, 13, 14) skeins

NEEDLES
US 7 (4.5mm) straight or circular needles, or size to obtain gauge
US 6 (4mm) DPNs or 16" circular needles, or one size smaller than size to obtain gauge

NOTIONS
Yarn Needle
Stitch Marker
Scrap Yarn or Stitch Holders
Spare Needle
25 (26, 27, 27, 29, 30)" Zipper
Matching Sewing Thread

GAUGE
19 sts and 27 rows = 4" in stockinette stitch, blocked
19 sts and 28 rows = 4" in Moss stitch, blocked

For pattern support, contact camomileknits@gmail.com

Alastair Vest

Notes:
A rugged yet cozy unisex vest designed to showcase beautiful wool yarns, this pattern incorporates several different textures to create a warm and breathable fabric appropriate for chilly winter hikes. The stitch patterns are simple enough for a beginner, but the interesting construction details (inset pockets, tubular bind off) will keep advanced knitters engaged.

The vest is knit flat in three pieces from the bottom up with minimal shaping, and is intended to be worn with 2-4" of positive ease. A seamed construction has been chosen to add stability and structure, with stitches picked up around the neck for the collar, and around the arms for a band of 1x1 Ribbing. There is a zip fastening at the front, with I-cord edging on either side.

Right Twist (RT)
K2tog, leaving the sts on the LH needle. K into the first st again and slide both off the needle.

Moss St (worked flat over an even number of sts)
Row 1 (RS): (K1, P1) to end.
Row 2 (WS): Rep Row 1.
Row 3: (P1, K1) to end.
Row 4: Rep Row 3.
Rep Rows 1-4 for pattern.

1x1 Rib (worked in the rnd over an even number of sts)
All Rnds: (K1, P1) to end.
Rep until desired length.

I-cord Edging
Row 1 (RS): K1, SL1 WYIF, K1.
Row 2 (WS): SL1 WYIF, K1, SL1 WYIF.

German Twisted Cast On
Leaving a long tail (about 0.5" for each st to be CO), make a slipknot and place on your needle (this is the first st). Place your thumb and forefinger between the yarn ends so that the working yarn is around your forefinger and the tail end is around your thumb. Bring the needle in front of the thumb, under both strands around the thumb, down into the center of the thumb loop, then forward. Now bring the needle over the strand going to your forefinger, then back through the loop on the thumb, turning the thumb slightly to make room for the needle to pass through. Drop the loop off the thumb and, placing the thumb back in the original position, tighten up the resulting st on the needle. Rep for the desired number of sts.

Tubular Bind Off
Break yarn and leave a long tail approximately 4 times the circumference of the armhole. Thread the working yarn onto a yarn needle and proceed as follows, being careful to maintain an even tension:

Put the yarn needle through the first st on the needle as if to K and SL the st off the needle. Put the yarn needle through the 2nd st on needle as if to P, do not slip off. Put the yarn needle through the first st on the needle as if to P and SL off the needle. From the back push the yarn needle between the first and 2nd sts on the needle, then from the front go into the 2nd st on the needle as if to K and push through to the back. Rep until all sts are bound off.

DIRECTIONS
All three pieces are worked flat from the bottom up.

Back Piece
With the larger needles and using the German Twisted Cast On, CO 92 (100, 108, 116, 124, 132) sts. Work the Mock Cable Rib hem as follows:
Row 1 (RS): SL1, P2, (K2, P2) until last st, K1.
Row 2 (WS): SL1, (K2, P2) until last 3 sts, K2, P1.
Row 3: SL1, P2, (RT, P2) until last st, K1.
Row 4: Rep Row 2.
Rep Rows 1-4 until work measures 4" from CO, ending with a WS row.
Cont in St st (K on RS, P on WS) with mock cable edging as follows:
Row 1 (RS): SL1, P2, K2, P1, St st until last 6 sts, P1, K2, P2, K1.
Row 2 (WS): SL1, K2, P2, K1, St st until last 6 sts, K1, P2, K2, P1.
Row 3: SL1, P2, RT, P1, St st until last 6 sts, P1, RT, P2, K1.
Row 4: Rep Row 2.
Rep these 4 rows until work measures 16.5 (17, 17.5, 18, 18.5, 19)" from the CO edge, ending on Row 4.

Armhole Shaping
BO 6 sts at the beginning of the next 2 rows. 80 (88, 96, 104, 112, 120) sts.
Cont in St st, BO 1 st at the beginning of each row until you have 68 (72, 80, 84, 92, 96) sts left on the needles.
Cont in St st until armhole measures 8.5 (9, 9.5, 10, 10.5, 11)".

Shoulder Shaping
BO 11 (11, 13, 13, 15, 15) sts at the beginning of the next 4 rows. Cut yarn, and put the remaining 24 (28, 28, 32, 32, 36) sts on a holder ready for the collar.

Right Front Piece (as worn)
Using the German Twisted Cast On, CO 46 (50, 54, 58, 62, 66) sts. Work the Mock Cable Rib hem as follows:
Row 1 (RS): K1, SL1 WYIF, K1, P2, (K2, P2) to last st, K1.
Row 2 (WS): SL1, (K2, P2) to last 5 sts, K2, SL1 WYIF, K1, SL1 WYIF.
Row 3: K1, SL1 WYIF, K1, P2, (RT, P2) to last st, K1.
Row 4: Rep Row 2.
Rep Rows 1-4 until work measures 4" from CO, ending with a WS row.

Cont in Moss St with mock cable/I-cord edging as follows:
Row 1 (RS): K1, SL1 WYIF, K1, P2, K2, P1, (K1, P1) to last 6 sts, P1, K2, P2, K1.
Row 2 (WS): SL1, K2, P2, K1, (K1, P1) to last 8 sts, K1, P2, K2, SL1 WYIF, K1, SL1 WYIF.
Row 3: K1, SL1 WYIF, K1, P2, RT, P1, (P1, K1) to last 6 sts, P1, RT, P2, K1.
Row 4: SL1, K2, P2, K1, (P1, K1) to last 8 sts, K1, P2, K2, SL1 WYIF, K1, SL1 WYIF.
Rep Rows 1-4 until work measures 5" from CO, ending on Row 4.

Pocket

Cont Row 1 as established to last 11 (15, 19, 23, 27, 31) sts. Put these sts on a holder and turn your work. Work as follows, beginning on Row 2:
Row 1 (RS): K1, SL1 WYIF, K1, P2, K2, P1, (K1, P1) to last st, K1.
Row 2 (WS): (P1, K1) to last 7 sts, P2, K2, SL1 WYIF, K1, SL1 WYIF.
Row 3: K1, SL1 WYIF, K1, P2, RT, P1, (P1, K1) to last st, P1.
Row 4: (K1, P1) to last 8 sts, K1, P2, K2, SL1 WYIF, K1, SL1 WYIF.
Rep Rows 1-4 until pocket measures 6", ending on Row 4. Place these sts on a holder and put the previously held sts on the needles.

Join new ball of yarn and CO 27 sts. Work as follows:
Row 1 (RS): K27, (P1, K1) to last 6 sts, P1, K2, P2, K1.
Row 2 (WS): SL1, K2, P2, K1, (K1, P1) to last 27 sts, P27.
Row 3: K27, (P1, K1) to last 6 sts, P1, RT, P2, K1.
Row 4: SL1, K2, P2, K1, (K1, P1) to last 27 sts, P27.
Rep Rows 1-4 until the back of the pocket measures 6", ending on Row 4. Cut yarn and put these sts onto a spare needle and return the front of the pocket to your needles.

Next Row (RS): K1, SL1 WYIF, K1, P2, K2, P1, hold spare needle behind work and work the next 27 sts tog in Moss St pattern, joining the front and back of the pocket. Cont in (K1, P1) to last 6 sts, P1, K2, P2, K1.
Cont in Moss St with mock cable/I-cord edging as previously established, beginning on Row 2, until work measures 16.5 (17, 17.5, 18, 18.5, 19)" from the CO edge, ending on Row 4.

Armhole Shaping

Work Row 1 once more. BO 6 sts at the beginning of Row 2. 40 (44, 48, 52, 56, 60) sts.
Work Row 3. Starting on Row 4, BO 1 st at the beginning of each WS row until you have 34 (36, 40, 42, 46, 48) sts left on the needles.
Row 1 (RS): K1, SL1 WYIF, K1, P2, K2, P1, (P1, K1) to end.
Row 2 (WS): (K1, P1) to last 8 sts, K1, P2, K2, SL1 WYIF, K1, SL1 WYIF.
Row 3: K1, SL1 WYIF, K1, P2, RT, P1, (P1, K1) to end.
Row 4: (K1, P1) to last 8 sts, K1, P2, K2, SL1 WYIF, K1, SL1 WYIF.
Cont in established pattern until armhole measures 6 (6.25, 6.75, 6.75, 7.25, 7.5)", ending on a WS row (make a note of whether you finish on Row 2 or Row 4, this will be relevant for working the collar).

Neck Shaping

Cut yarn and with RS facing put the first 8 sts of the next row on a holder ready for the collar. Join a new ball of yarn and cont in Moss st pattern for 2 rows. BO 2 sts at the beginning of next 2 (3, 3, 4, 4, 5) RS rows. 22 (22, 26, 26, 30, 30) sts remaining.
Cont in Moss St pattern until armhole measures 8.5 (9, 9.5, 10, 10.5, 11)".

Shoulder Shaping
BO 11 (11, 13, 13, 15, 15) sts at the beginning of the next 2 WS rows. 0 sts remain. Cut yarn, leaving a long tail for seaming.

Left Front Piece (as worn)
Using the German Twisted Cast On, CO 46 (50, 54, 58, 62, 66) sts. Work the Mock Cable Rib hem as follows:
Row 1 (RS): SL1, (P2, K2) to last 5 sts, P2, K1, SL1 WYIF, K1.
Row 2 (WS): SL1 WYIF, K1, SL1 WYIF, K2, (P2, K2) to last st, K1.
Row 3: SL1, (P2, RT) to last 5 sts, P2, K1, SL1 WYIF, K1.
Row 4: Rep Row 2.
Rep Rows 1-4 until work measures 4" from CO.
Cont in Moss St with mock cable/I-cord edging as follows:
Row 1 (RS): SL1, P2, K2, P1, (K1, P1) to last 8 sts, P1, K2, P2, K1, SL1 WYIF, K1.
Row 2 (WS): SL1 WYIF, K1, SL1 WYIF, K2, P2, K1, (K1, P1) to last 5 sts, P2, K2, K1.
Row 3: SL1, P2, RT, P1, (P1, K1) to last 8 sts, P1, RT, P2, K1, SL1 WYIF, K1.
Row 4: SL1 WYIF, K1, SL1 WYIF, K2, P2, K1, (P1, K1) to last 5 sts, P2, K2, K1.
Rep Rows 1-4 until work measures 5" from CO, ending on Row 4.

Pocket
Cont working Row 1 as established for the first 11 (15, 19, 23, 27, 31) sts and put the remaining 35 sts on a holder. CO 27 sts and work as follows, beginning on Row 2:
Row 1 (RS): SL1, P2, K2, P1, (P1, K1) to last 27 sts, K27.
Row 2 (WS): P27, (K1, P1) to last 6 sts, K1, P2, K2, K1.
Row 3: SL1, P2, RT, P1, (P1, K1) to last 27 sts, K27.
Row 4: P27, (K1, P1) to last 6 sts, K1, P2, K2, K1.
Rep Rows 1-4 until the back of the pocket measures 6", ending on Row 4.
Put these sts on a holder, return previously held sts to your needles and work as follows:
Row 1 (RS): (P1, K1), to last 8 sts, P1, K2, P2, K1, SL1 WYIF, K1.
Row 2 (WS): SL1 WYIF, K1, SL1 WYIF, K2, P2, K1, (K1, P1) to end.
Row 3: (P1, K1), to last 8 sts, P1, RT, P2, K1, SL1 WYIF, K1.
Row 4: SL1 WYIF, K1, SL1 WYIF, K2, P2, K1, (K1, P1) to end.
Rep Rows 1-4 until pocket measures 6", ending on Row 4.
Cut yarn and put these sts onto a spare needle. Return the previously held sts to the working needles.
Next Row (RS): SL1, P2, K2, (P1, K1) to last 27 sts. Hold spare needle in front of work and work the next 27 sts tog in Moss St pattern, joining the front and back of the pocket. Work the remaining 8 sts from the spare needle as P1, K2, P2, K1, SL1 WYIF, K1.
Cont in Moss St with mock cable/I-cord edging as previously established, beginning on Row 2, until work measures 16.5 (17, 17.5, 18, 18.5, 19)" from the CO edge, ending on Row 4.

Armhole Shaping
BO 6 sts at the beginning of Row 1. 40 (44, 48, 52, 56, 60) sts. Work Row 2, then starting with Row 3 BO 1 st at the beginning of each RS row until you have 34 (36, 40, 42, 46, 48) sts left on the needles.

20 Alastair Vest

Row 1 (RS): (K1, P1) to last 8 sts, P1, K2, P2, K1, SL1 WYIF, K1.
Row 2 (WS): SL1 WYIF, K1, SL1 WYIF, K2, P2, K1 (K1, P1) to end.
Row 3: (P1, K1) to last 8 sts P1, RT, P2, K1, SL1 WYIF, K1.
Row 4: SL1 WYIF, K1, SL1 WYIF, K2, P2, K1 (P1, K1) to end.
Cont in established pattern until armhole measures 6 (6.25, 6.75, 6.75, 7.25, 7.5)", ending on a WS row (make sure you finish on the same row as the right front piece).

Neck Shaping
Turn your work and cont in Moss St pattern to the last 8 sts; put these sts on a holder ready for the collar and turn your work to the WS, cont in Moss St pattern for 2 more rows. BO 2 sts at the beginning of next 2 (3, 3, 4, 4, 5) WS rows, until you have 22 (22, 26, 26, 30, 30) sts remaining.
Cont in Moss St pattern until armhole measures 8.5 (9, 9.5, 10, 10.5, 11)".

Shoulder Shaping
BO 11 (11, 13, 13, 15, 15) sts at the beginning of the next 2 RS rows. 0 sts remain. Cut yarn, leaving a long tail for seaming.

Seaming
Sew up the pockets using the left-over yarn tails. Wash and block your pieces to the diagram dimensions, taking care not to stretch the pockets out of shape or drop any sts that are on holders. Seam body using Mattress st, and at the shoulders using Whip st.

Collar
Put the 8 collar sts from the left front piece onto your needle. Moving in a counter-clockwise direction around the collar PU and K 14 (16, 18, 20, 22, 24) sts, then put the 24 (28, 28, 32, 32, 36) held sts from the back piece onto the needle. Continuing in a counter-clockwise direction, PU and K a further 14 (16, 18, 20, 22, 24) sts and then put the 8 neck sts from the right front piece onto your needle. 68 (76, 80, 88, 92, 100) sts. Join yarn on the RS and work as follows (beginning on either Row 1 or Row 3 depending on which row you finished on for the neck shaping):
Row 1 (RS): K1, SL1 WYIF, K1, P2, (K2, P2) to last 3 sts, K1, SL1 WYIF, K1.
Row 2 (WS): SL1 WYIF, K1, SL1 WYIF, (K2, P2) to last 5 sts, K2, SL1 WYIF, K1, SL1 WYIF.
Row 3: K1, SL1 WYIF, K1, P2, (RT, P2) to last 3 sts, K1, SL1 WYIF, K1.
Row 4: Rep Row 2.
Rep Rows 1-4, until collar measures 3 (3, 3, 3, 4, 4)".
BO loosely in pattern.

Armhole Ribbing
With the smaller needles, PU and K 76 (80, 86, 90, 96, 100) sts around the armhole. PM and join for working in the rnd. Work in 1x1 Rib until the band measures 0.75". BO using the Tubular Bind Off, or your preferred stretchy method. Rep for the second armhole.

Finishing
Weave in remaining ends, wash, and gently block collar and armhole ribbing. Attach zipper to front pieces using Whip st and sewing thread.

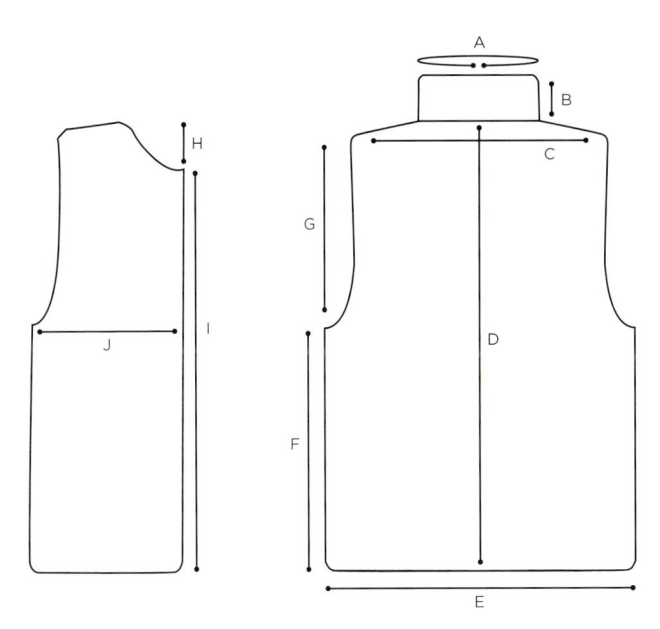

A: 14.25 (16, 16.75, 18.5, 19.25, 21)"
B: 3 (3, 3, 3, 4, 4)"
C: 14.25 (15.25, 16.75, 17.75, 19.25, 20.25)"
D: 25 (26, 27, 28, 29, 30)"
E: 19 (20.75, 22.25, 24, 25.75, 27.25)"
F: 16.5 (17, 17.5, 18, 18.5, 19)"
G: 8.5 (9, 9.5, 10, 10.5, 11)"
H: 2.5 (2.75, 2.75, 3.25, 3.25, 3.5)"
I: 22.5 (23.25, 24.25, 24.75, 25.75, 26.5)"
J: 9.5 (10.25, 11.25, 12, 12.75, 13.75)"

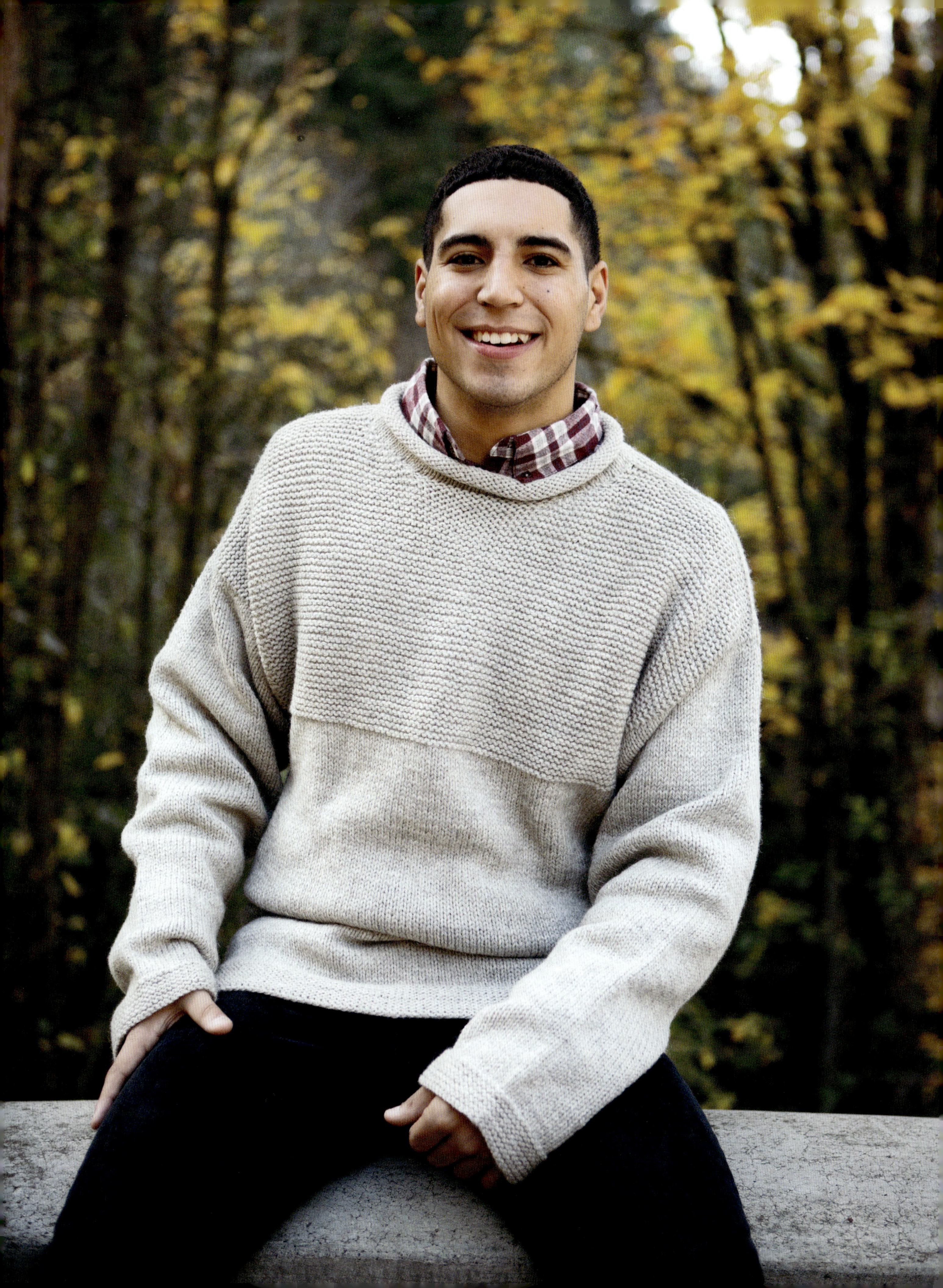

BARGEMAN

by Todd Gocken

FINISHED MEASUREMENTS
34.25 (38.25, 42.25, 46.25, 50.25, 54.25)" finished bust measurement; garment is meant to be worn with 2" of ease

YARN
Knit Picks Simply Wool (bulky weight, 100% Eco Wool; 193 yards/100g): Winkle 27481, 6 (7, 8, 9, 10, 11) hanks

NEEDLES
US 9 (5.5mm) circular needles plus DPNs, or two 24" circular needles for two circulars technique, or one 32" or longer circular needle for Magic Loop technique, or size to obtain gauge
US 6 (4mm) DPNs or two 24" circular needles for two circulars technique, or one 32" or longer circular needle for Magic Loop technique, or 2 sizes smaller than size to obtain gauge

NOTIONS
Yarn Needle
Stitch Markers
Scrap Yarn or Stitch holder
Spare DPNs

GAUGE
18 sts and 28 rows = 4" in stockinette stitch in the round on larger needles, blocked
18 sts and 36 rows = 4" in garter stitch on larger needles, blocked

For pattern support, contact todd@toddgockendesigns.com

Bargeman

Notes:
This unisex sweater exemplifies the classic Gansey distilled to its most simple and elemental form. It utilizes traditional Gansey construction: knit in the round from the bottom up, with the front and back upper body knit flat and joined at the shoulders with a 3-Needle Bind Off, the stitches for the sleeves are then picked up around the armholes and are knit down to the cuffs. The welt and cuffs are knit in garter stitch, as is the yoke. The collar is knit in stockinette stitch with a rolled edge. This garment is completely seamless and is created without any purl stitches.

3-Needle Bind Off
A tutorial for the 3-Needle Bind Off can be found at https://tutorials.knitpicks.com/3-needle-bind-off/.

Sewn Bind Off
A tutorial for the Sewn Bind Off can be found at https://tutorials.knitpicks.com/sewn-bind-off/.

Garter Stitch (worked flat over any number of sts)
All Rows: Knit across.

DIRECTIONS

Welt/Hem (make 2 the same)
The welt (hem) is made in two parts to create side vents. Using larger circular needles, CO 77 (86, 95, 104, 113, 122) sts. Work flat in garter stitch for 2 (2, 2, 2, 2.5, 2.5)", slipping the first st of every row. Make second welt identical to first.

Body
Place both welts onto one larger circular needle, separated by a M, PM, join in the rnd. 154 (172, 190, 208, 226, 244) sts.
Rnd 1: K all.
Rep this rnd until work reaches 16" from CO.

Gussets
Gussets are created at the underarms of the sweater.
Rnd 1: *SM, M1, PM, K to next M, rep from * once more. 2 sts inc.
Rnd 2: K all.
Rnd 3: *SM, M1R, K to next M, M1L, SM, rep from * once more. 4 sts inc.
Rep Rnds 2-3 4 (5, 6, 7, 8, 8) more times. 11 (13, 15, 17, 19, 19) sts between Ms.
Rep Rnd 2 once more, placing the gusset sts on scrap yarn.

Back
Row 1: Turn work, SL1, K across back to next gusset M. 77 (86, 95, 104, 113, 122) sts.
Rep this row, continuing to work flat in garter st for 84 (88, 92, 96, 100, 104) more rows, ending on a RS Row. Do not break yarn, do not BO.

Front
With WS facing, join new ball at right front, K to end of row.
Row 1: Turn work, SL1, K across back to next gusset M. 77 (86, 95, 104, 113, 122) sts.
Rep this row, continuing to work flat in garter st for 68 (72, 76, 78, 82, 84) more rows, ending on a WS row.

Neck Shaping
Left Shoulder
Row 1 (RS): SL1, K31 (35, 39, 43, 47, 51). Turn work. Work left shoulder over these 32 (36, 40, 44, 48, 52) sts only.
Row 2 (WS): SSK, K to end of row. 1 st dec.
Row 3 (RS): K to 3 sts before end of row, K2tog, K1. 1 st dec.
Rep Rows 2-3 until 26 (28, 30, 34, 38, 42) sts remain. Work 10 (10, 8, 10, 10, 12) more rows without decreases, slipping the first st of each row and ending on a RS row. Using the working yarn from the back, and with WSs together, join left shoulder to back using a 3-Needle Bind Off, break yarn.

Right Shoulder
With RS facing, SL next 13 (14, 15, 16, 17, 18) sts from the front neck onto a stitch holder or scrap yarn, join new ball, K to end of row. 32 (36, 40, 44, 48, 52) sts. Turn work.
Row 1 (WS): SL1, K to 3 sts before end of row, K2tog, K1. 1 st dec.
Row 2 (RS): SSK, K to end of row. 1 st dec.

Rep Rows 1-2 until 26 (28, 30, 34, 38, 42) sts remain. Work 10 (10, 8, 10, 10, 12) more rows without decreases, slipping the first st of each row and ending on a RS row. Using the working yarn from the right front, and with WSs together, join right shoulder to back using a 3-Needle Bind Off. Do not break yarn. 25 (30, 35, 36, 37, 38) live back neck sts remain.

Collar
Using working yarn from the right shoulder and with RS facing and larger needles, K25 (30, 35, 36, 37, 38) across back neck, PU and K 17 (16, 15, 17, 18, 20) sts from left neck, K 13 (14, 15, 16, 17, 18) held sts from the front neck, PU and K 17 (16, 15, 17, 18, 20) sts from right neck, PM, join in the rnd. 72 (76, 80, 86, 90, 96) sts.
Rnd 1: K all.
Rep Rnd 1 until neck reaches 2".
Switch to smaller size needle.
Rep Rnd 1 for 1" additional.
BO very loosely using Sewn Bind Off.

Left Sleeve
With RS facing, join yarn at right side of gusset.
Using larger needles, K across held gusset sts, PM, PU and K 42 (44, 46, 48, 50, 52) sts from left front (every st of the slipped st selvage), PU and K 42 (44, 46, 48, 50, 52) sts from left back, (every st of the slipped st selvage), PM, join in the rnd. 95 (101, 107, 113, 119, 123) sts.
Rnd 1: SSK, K across gusset to 2 sts before M, K2tog, K to end of rnd. 2 sts dec.
Rnd 2: K all sts.
Rep Rnds 1-2 until 3 sts are left of the gusset.
Next Rnd: SM, K2tog, K1, SM, K to end of rnd. 1 st dec.
Next Rnd: SM, SSK, remove M, K to end of rnd. 85 (89, 93, 97, 101, 105) sts.
Dec Rnd: K2tog, K to last 2 sts, SSK. 2 sts dec.
Work a Dec Rnd every 4th rnd a total of 3 (6, 10, 8, 8, 10) times, then work a Dec Rnd every 5th rnd 19 (17, 14, 16, 17, 16) more times. 41 (43, 45, 49, 51, 53) sts remaining. Cont working without decreases until the sleeve reaches 17.5 (18, 18.5, 19, 20, 20.5)".

Cuff
The cuff is worked flat. Turn work, ready to begin a WS row. Work in garter st for a total of 1 (1.5, 1.5, 1.5, 2, 2)", creating a garter st cuff.
BO all sts.

Right Sleeve
Work as for Left Sleeve, picking up sts from right back, (every st of the slipped st selvage), and from right front, (every st of the slipped st selvage).

Finishing
Weave in ends, wash, and block to diagram.

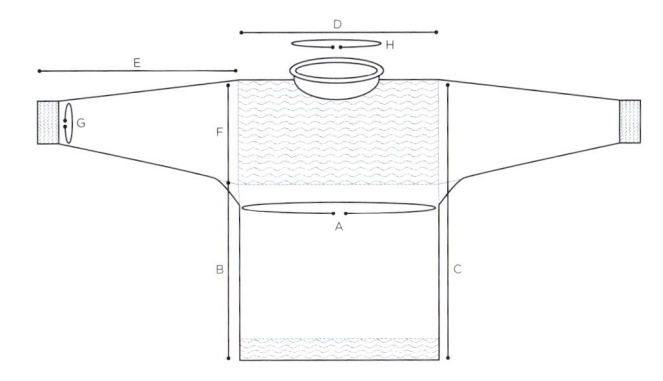

A: 34.25 (38.25, 42.25, 46.25, 50.25, 54.25)"
B: 17.5 (17.75, 18.25, 18.5, 18.75, 18.85)"
C: 27 (27.5, 28.5, 29, 29.75, 30.25)"
D: 17 (19, 21, 23, 25, 27)"
E: 18.5 (19.5, 20, 20.5, 22, 22.5)"
F: 9.25 (9.75, 10.25, 10.75, 11, 11.5)"
G: 9 (9.25, 9.75, 10.75, 11, 11.5)"
H: 16 (17, 17.75, 19, 20, 21.25)"

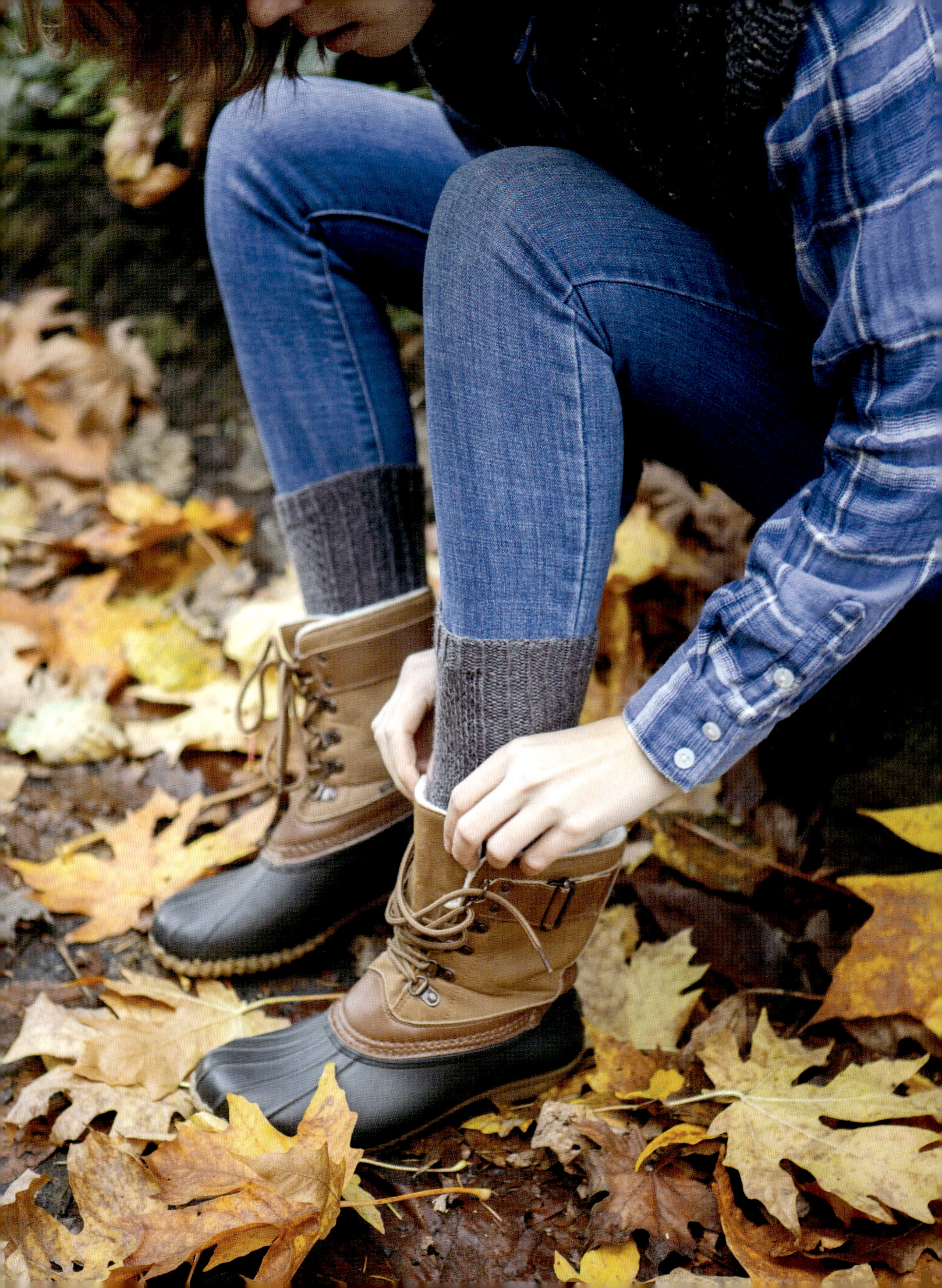

EYE OF PARTRIDGE HIKING SOCKS

by ND

FINISHED MEASUREMENTS
7.5 (8.25, 9)" leg and foot circumference

YARN
Knit Picks Stroll (fingering weight, 75% Fine Superwash Merino Wool, 25% Nylon; 231 yards/50g): Basalt Heather 24593, 2 skeins

NEEDLES
US 1 (2.5mm) 32" or longer circular needles for Magic Loop technique or DPNs, or size to obtain gauge

NOTIONS
Yarn Needle
4 Stitch Markers

GAUGE
32 sts and 44 rows = 4" in stockinette stitch in the round, blocked

For pattern support, contact knotspurls@gmail.com

Eye of Partridge Hiking Socks

Notes:

These socks are worked in the round from the cuff down, with a heel flap and gusset. The ribbing and Eye of Partridge patterns are worked over both front and back to the heel, then continued over the top of the foot to the toe; the insole is worked in stockinette stitch.

When slipping sts, hold yarn in back for K sts, and in front for P sts.

Eye of Partridge Pattern (in the rnd over an even number of sts)
Rnd 1: (SL1, K1) to end.
Rnds 2, 4: K all sts.
Rnd 3: (K1, SL1) to end.
Rep Rnds 1-4 for pattern.
When working over an odd number of sts, end Rnd 1 with SL1 and Rnd 3 with K1.

Eye of Partridge Pattern (worked flat over an even number of sts)
Row 1: (SL1, K1) across.
Rows 2, 4: P across.
Row 3: (K1, SL1) across.
Rep Rows 1-4 for pattern.
When working over an odd number of sts, end Row 1 with SL1 and Row 3 with K1.

DIRECTIONS

CO 60 (66, 72) sts, loosely. Join in the rnd and PM, being careful not to twist sts.

Cuff
Begin half-twisted rib:
Rnd 1: (P1, K1TBL, P1) to end.
Rep Rnd 1 for 1", or until desired Cuff rib length.

Leg
Rnd 1: *Work 8 sts in established rib, K14 (17, 20), work 8 sts in rib; rep from * 1 time.
Rnd 2: *Work 8 sts in established rib, work Eye of Partridge pattern (in the rnd) over next 14 (17, 20) sts, work 8 sts in rib; rep from * 1 time.
Rep Rnd 2 until Leg measures 6" from CO, or desired length.

Heel

Heel Flap
The heel flap is worked flat over 30 (33, 36) sts.
When working half-twisted rib on WS rows, work K sts TFL, and P sts TBL.
Row 1: Work 8 sts in established rib, work Eye of Partridge pattern (flat) over next 14 (17, 20) sts, work 8 sts in rib, turn.
Row 2: SL1, work 7 sts in rib, work Eye of Partridge pattern (flat) over next 14 (17, 20) sts, work 8 sts in rib, turn.
Rep Row 2 28 (30, 32) more times.

Turn Heel
Row 1 (RS): SL1, K17 (19, 21), SSK, K1, turn.
Row 2 (WS): SL1, P7 (8, 9), P2tog, P1, turn.
Row 3: SL1, K to 1 st before gap, SSK, K1, turn.
Row 4: SL1, P to 1 st before gap, P2tog, P1, turn.
Rep Rows 3-4 until all heel sts are worked. For sizes 7.25" and 9", end the last 2 rows with SSK and P2tog, respectively.

Gusset
Begin working in the rnd again.
Rnd 1: SL1, K across heel sts, PU and K 15 (16, 17) sts along the edge of the heel flap, PM, work 30 (33, 36) front sts in established patterns, PM, PU and K 15 (16, 17) sts along the edge of the heel flap.
Rnd 2: K to 2 sts before M, K2tog, SM, work front sts in established patterns, SM, SSK, K to end.
Rnd 3: K to M, SM, work front sts in patterns, SM, K to end.
Rep Rnds 2-3 until there are 30 (33, 36) insole sts, 60 (66, 72) sts total.

Foot
Rnd 1: K to M, work front sts in established patterns to M, K to end.
Rep Rnd 1 until foot measures 2 (2, 2.25)" shorter than desired length from the back of heel.

Toe
Rnd 1: K to 3 sts before M, K2tog, K1, SM, K1, SSK, work front sts in patterns to 3 sts before M, K2tog, K1, SM, K1, SSK, K to end. 4 sts dec.
Rnd 2: K to M, SM, K2, work front sts in patterns to 2 sts before M, K2, SM, K to end.
Rep Rnds 1-2 a total of 8 (9, 10) times until 24 (26, 28) sts remain.
Rep Rnd 1 only 3 more times until 12 (14, 16) sts remain; 6 (7, 8) each front and back.
K to first M.
Graft remaining toe sts together using Kitchener St.

Finishing
Weave in ends and block.

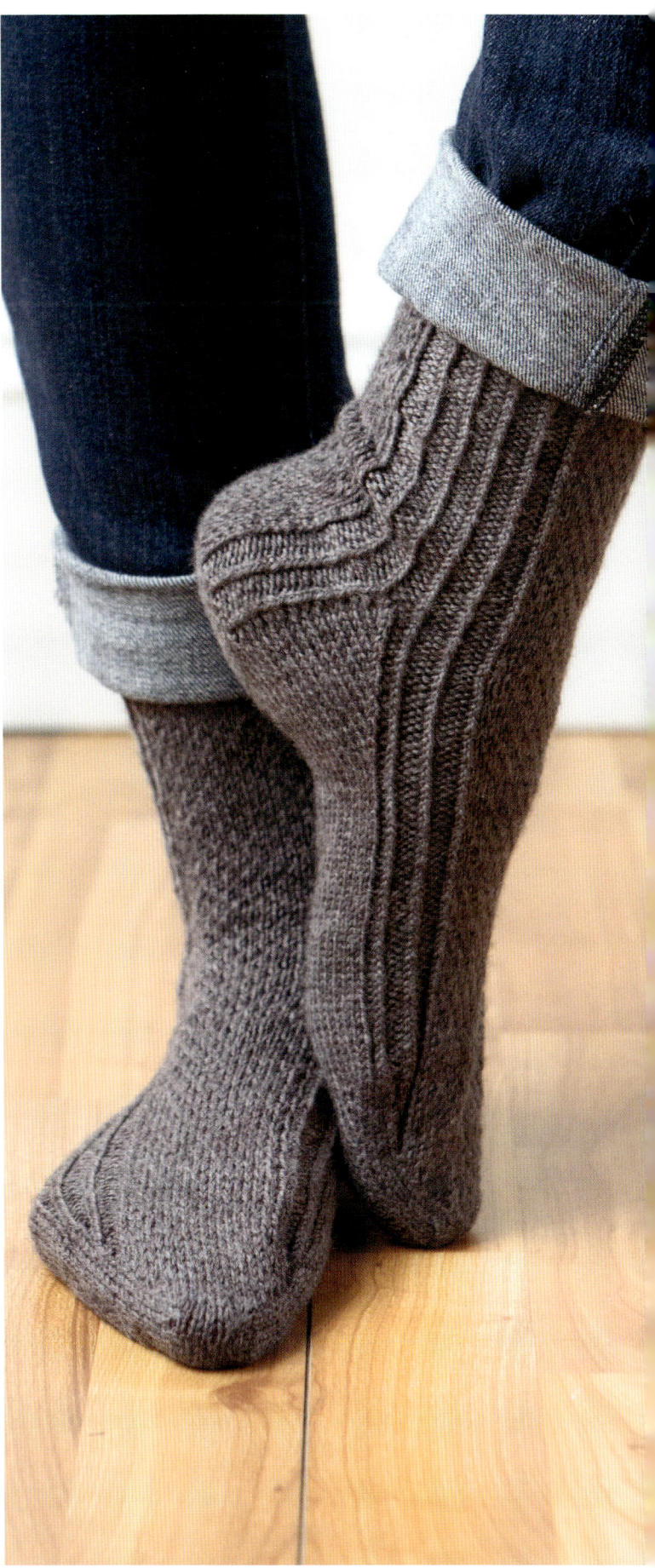

Eye of Partridge Hiking Socks 29

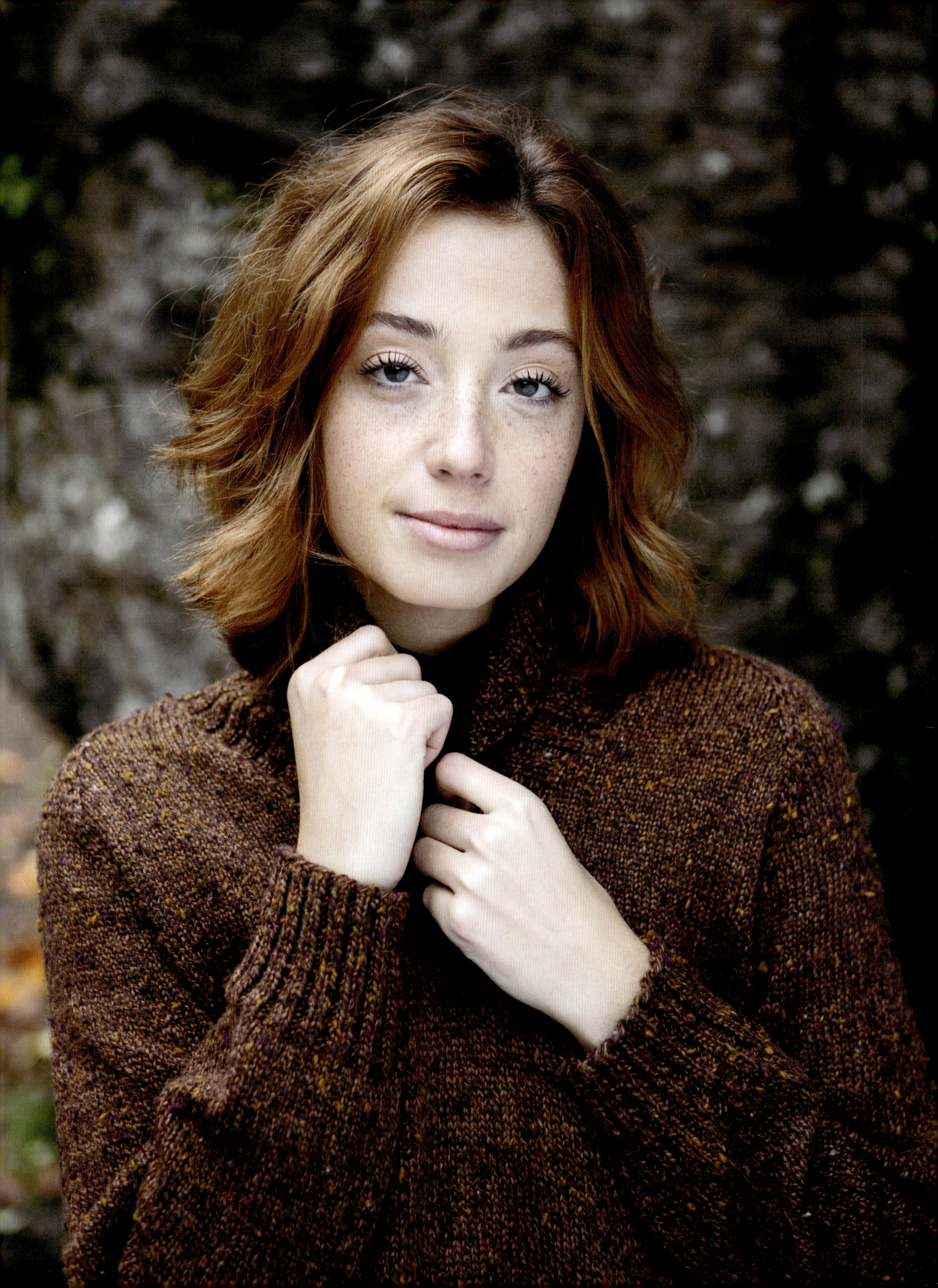

HURRICANE RIDGE PULLOVER

by Allison Griffith

FINISHED MEASUREMENTS
34.75 (39, 41.75, 46, 50, 54.25, 57, 61.25, 65.5)" finished bust measurement; garment is meant to be worn with 2-4" of positive ease

YARN
Knit Picks Provincial Tweed (worsted weight, 80% Superwash Fine Highland Wool, 20% Donegal; 250 yards/100g): MC Coffee Bean 27581, 5 (5, 6, 6, 7, 7, 8, 8, 8) hanks

NEEDLES
US 5 (3.75mm) DPNs and circular needles, or size to obtain gauge

US 4 (3.5mm) DPNs and circular needles, or one size smaller than size to obtain gauge

NOTIONS
Yarn Needle
Stitch Markers
Scrap Yarn or Stitch Holders

GAUGE
23 sts and 30 rows = 4" in stockinette stitch in the round on larger needles, blocked

Hurricane Ridge Pullover

Notes:

The Hurricane Ridge Pullover is the perfect casual sweater to accompany you on your adventures, whether you're hiking the Pacific Crest Trail or walking around the corner to your favorite coffee shop. A relaxed silhouette and positive ease combines with a shawl collar, raglan shoulders, and a hip-length split hem to create a comfortable and classic garment.

The Hurricane Ridge Pullover is worked seamlessly, from the bottom up. The split hem is worked flat (front and back separately), before being joined and worked in the round to the armpits. Arms are worked separately, then joined to the body. After a few rounds of yoke, stitches are bound off for the front neck, and the sweater is worked back and forth, simultaneously working raglan shaping and decreasing at the neck opening. After binding off at the back of the neck, the collar is picked up and worked back and forth with short row shaping to create a generous shawl collar. The ends of the collar are then sewn in place along the front of the neck.

Wrap and Turn (W&T)

A tutorial for the Wrap and Turn (W&T) can be found at http://tutorials.knitpicks.com/wptutorials/short-rows-wrap-and-turn-or-wt/.

Kitchener Stitch

A tutorial for the Kitchener Stitch can be found at http://tutorials.knitpicks.com/wptutorials/kitchener-stitch/.

DIRECTIONS
Body

The hem is worked flat in two pieces from the bottom up, then joined and the body is worked in the round to the underarms.

Hem Front

With smaller circular needle, loosely CO 100 (112, 120, 132, 144, 156, 164, 176, 188) sts.

Row 1 (WS): K3 (P2, K2) to 1 before end, K1.
Row 2 (RS): P3 (K2, P2) to 1 before end, P1.

Work Rows 1 and 2 until Hem Front measures 3" from CO edge (or desired length), ending with a RS row. Break yarn and transfer to scrap yarn or stitch holder. Set aside.

Hem Back

Work as for Hem Front until Hem Back measures 5" from CO edge (or desired length), ending with a RS row. Do not break yarn. Cont to Main Body.

Main Body

With the same needle that was used for the Hem Back, work the next RS row of Hem Front over held sts, following the established pattern. PM. The Body is worked in the rnd from now on. 200 (224, 240, 264, 288, 312, 328, 352, 376) sts.

Rnd 1: (K1, P2, K1) around.

Rep Rnd 1 until piece measures 1" from join.

Switch to larger circular needle and K all rnds (St st) until sweater measures 18 (18, 18, 19, 19, 19, 20, 20, 20)" from Front CO edge, or desired length.

K 10 (11, 12, 13, 14, 15, 16, 17, 19) sts of the next row. Transfer to scrap yarn or st holder, keeping marker in place. Set aside.

Sleeves (make 2 the same)

The sleeves are worked in the rnd from the cuff up.

With smaller DPNs, loosely CO 44 (56, 60, 64, 72, 76, 80, 88, 92) sts. PM for beginning of rnd (center of underarm).

Rnd 1: (K2, P2) around.

Rep Rnd 1 until piece measures 3" from CO edge.

Switch to larger DPNs and K (St st) for 6 (8, 7, 6, 6, 5, 5, 5, 4) rnds. Work Increase Rnd as follows:

Increase Rnd: K1, inc 1, K to 1 before M, inc 1, K1. 2 sts inc.

Cont in St st, working an Inc Rnd every 7 (9, 8, 7, 7, 6, 6, 6, 5)th rnd, until you have worked a total of 13 (11, 12, 14, 14, 17, 17, 18, 20) Inc Rnds. 70 (78, 84, 92, 100, 110, 114, 124, 132) sts.

Cont in St st without shaping until sleeve measures 17.5 (17.5, 17.5, 18.5, 18.5, 18.5, 19.5, 19.5, 19.5)" from CO edge or desired length.

First sleeve only (Left Sleeve): K 10 (11, 12, 13, 14, 15, 16, 17, 19) sts of the next row. Transfer to scrap yarn or st holder. Break yarn and set aside.

Second sleeve only (Right Sleeve): K 10 (11, 12, 13, 14, 15, 16, 17, 19) sts of the next row. Do not break yarn. Cont to Yoke.

Yoke

The Sleeves and Body are joined, then worked in the rnd to the base of the neck. Sts are then bound off at the center of the neck, and the remainder of the Yoke is worked flat.

Join Sleeves and Body

With larger circular needle, K across Right Sleeve to 10 (11, 12, 13, 14, 15, 16, 17, 19) sts before end of rnd. Place Back Right M. Transfer remaining 20 (22, 24, 26, 28, 30, 32, 34, 38) sleeve sts to scrap yarn or st holder, removing M. K 80 (90, 96, 106, 116, 126, 132, 142, 150) sts across the back Body. Place Back Left M. Transfer the next 20 (22, 24, 26, 28, 30, 32, 34, 38) Body sts to scrap yarn or st holder. K across Left Sleeve to 10 (11, 12, 13, 14, 15, 16, 17, 19) sts before end of rnd. Place Front Left M. Transfer remaining 20 (22, 24, 26, 28, 30, 32, 34, 38) sleeve sts to scrap yarn or st holder, removing M. K 80 (90, 96, 106, 116, 126, 132, 142, 150) sts across the Front Body. Place Front Right M (end of rnd). Transfer the remaining 20 (22, 24, 26, 28, 30, 32, 34, 38) Body sts to scrap yarn or st holder, removing M. 260 (292, 312, 344, 376, 412, 428, 464, 488) sts.

Knit 3 rnds without shaping.

K to Front Left M, SM, K 34 (38, 41, 46, 50, 55, 58, 63, 67), BO 12 (14, 14, 14, 16, 16, 16, 16, 16) front neck sts. From now on, the Yoke is worked flat, beginning with a RS row.

Work Shoulders and Neckline

Row 1 (RS): (K to 2 before next M, K2tog, SM, SSK) 4 times, K to end. 8 sts dec.

Row 2 and 4 (WS): P across, slipping Ms.

Row 3 (RS): K1, SSK, (K to 2 before next M, K2tog, SM, SSK) 4 times, K to 3 before end, K2tog, K1. 10 sts dec.

Hurricane Ridge Pullover 33

Work Rows 1-4 a total of 11 (12, 13, 15, 16, 18, 18, 20, 21) times. 50 (62, 64, 60, 72, 72, 88, 88, 94) sts.
Work Rows 1-2 0 (1, 1, 0, 0, 0, 1, 0, 0) times (omit if 0). 50 (54, 56, 60, 72, 72, 80, 88, 94) sts.
BO.

Collar

The Collar is picked up along the neckline and worked flat with short row shaping.

With the smaller circular needle and RS facing evenly PU and K 108 (120, 128, 140, 156, 168, 176, 192, 204) sts along the neckline, beginning on the RH side of the neckline next to the BO sts, and ending on the left. Do not pick up any sts along the 12 (14, 14, 14, 16, 16, 16, 16, 16) BO sts at the center of the neckline.

Setup Row (WS): P3, K2, P2, K1, (K1, P2, K1, PM) 4 times, (K1, P2, K1) to 24 sts before end, (PM, K1, P2, K1) 4 times, K1, P2, K2, P3.

Begin short row shaping to create the collar, continuing the ribbing as established.

Rows 1-2: Work to last M, SM, W&T.
Rows 3-4: Work to third to last M, SM, W&T.
Rows 5-6: Work to end.
Rows 7-8: Work to second to last M, SM, W&T.
Rows 9-10: Work to fourth to last M, SM, W&T.
Rows 11-12: Work to end.

Rep Rows 1-12 5 (5, 5, 5, 6, 6, 6, 6, 6) times. Then rep Rows 1-6 0 (1, 1, 1, 0, 0, 0, 0, 0) times (omit if 0).
BO very loosely.

Finishing

Sew edges of the collar neatly to the BO sts in the center of the neck, overlapping the ends.
Close underarm openings with Kitchener Stitch.
Weave in ends, wash, and block to diagram.

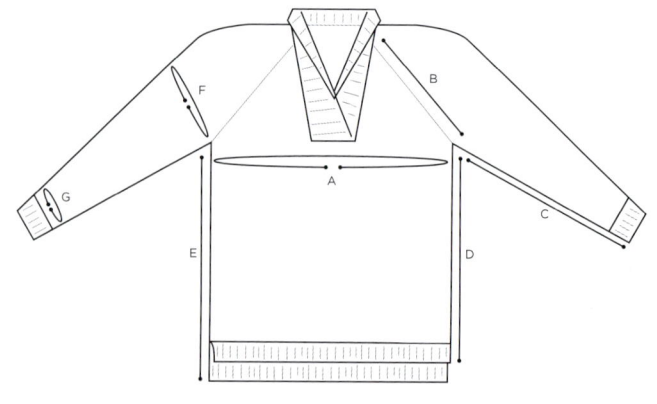

A: 34.75 (39, 41.75, 46, 50, 54.25, 57, 61.25, 65.5)"
B: 6.5 (7.25, 7.75, 8.5, 9, 10.25, 10.5, 11.25, 11.75)"
C: 17.5 (17.5, 17.5, 18.5, 18.5, 18.5, 19.5, 19.5, 19.5)"
D: 18 (18, 18, 19, 19, 19, 20, 20, 20)"
E: 20 (20, 20, 21, 21, 21, 22, 22, 22)"
F: 12.25 (13.5, 14.5, 16, 17.25, 19, 19.75, 21.5, 23)"
G: 7.5 (9.75, 10.5, 11, 12.5, 13.25, 14, 15.25, 16)"

Hurricane Ridge Pullover

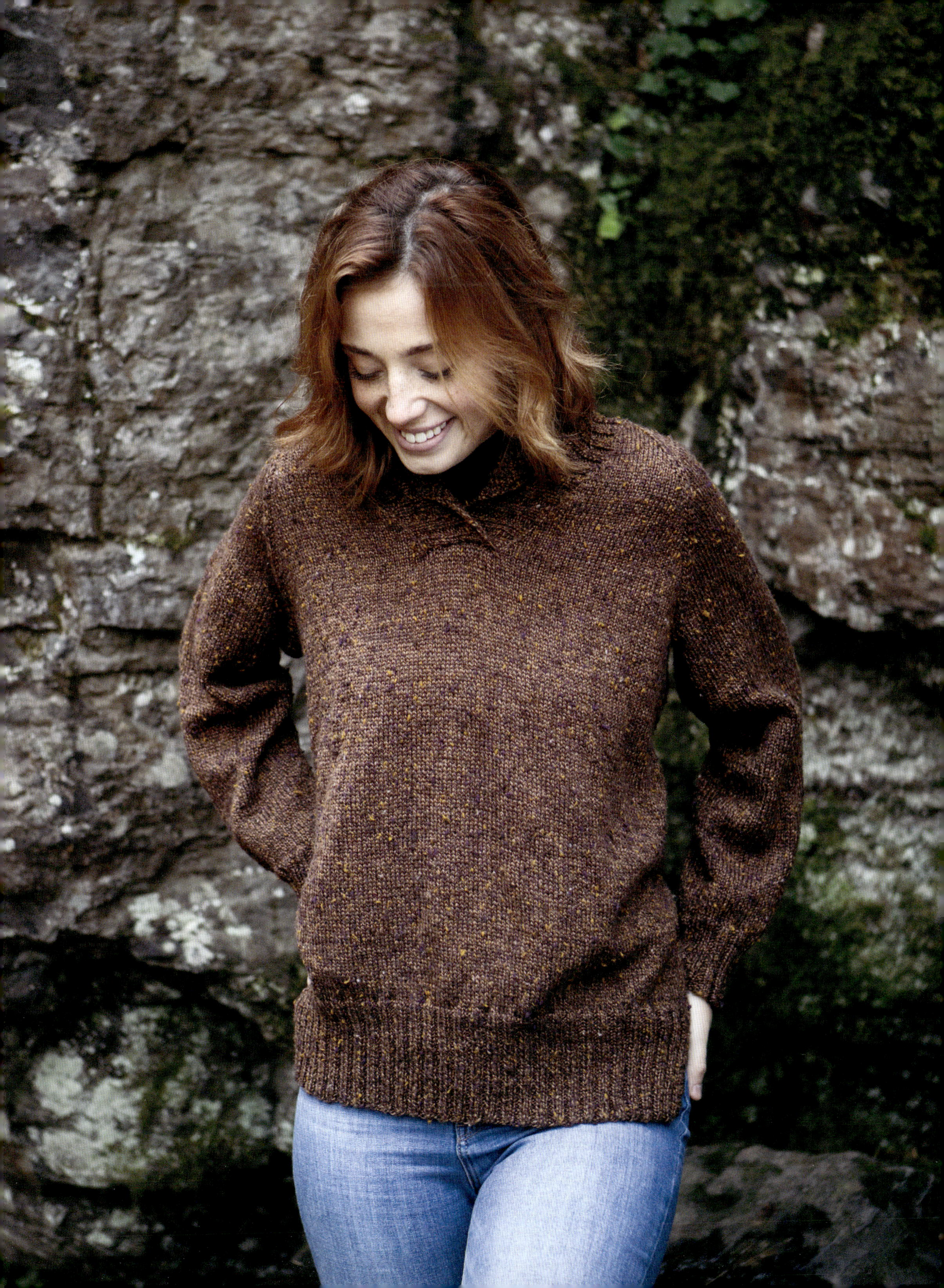

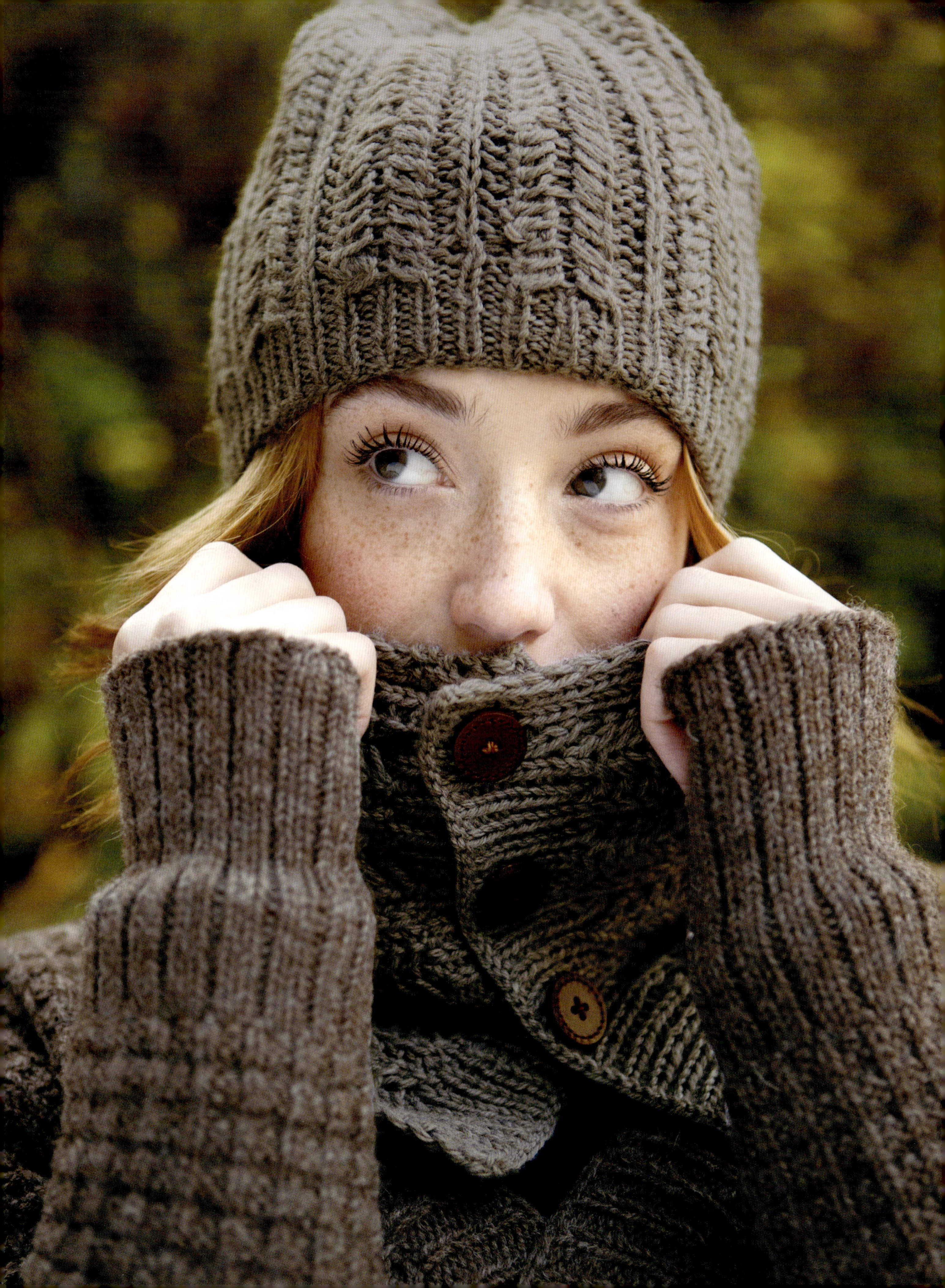

KAI HAT, COWL, AND LONG SCARF

by Tetiana Otruta

FINISHED MEASUREMENTS

Hat: 15.75 (17.25, 18.75)" circumference x 8.5 (9.25, 9.75)" high; to fit 20.5-21 (21.5-22.5, 23-24.5)" head circumference
Small Cowl (large cowl, long scarf): 9" wide x 23.5" circumference (43.5" circumference, 71" long)

YARN

Knit Picks Swish (worsted weight, 100% Fine Superwash Merino Wool); 110 yards/50g): Squirrel Heather 24090; hat, 2 skeins; small cowl (large cowl, long scarf), 2 (4, 6) skeins

NEEDLES

US 7 (4.5mm) DPNs or two 24" circular needles for two circulars technique, or one 32" or longer circular needle for Magic Loop technique, or size to obtain gauge (largest needle, for Hat and Cowl/Scarf body)

US 4 (3.5mm) DPNs or two 24" circular needles for two circulars technique, or one 32" or longer circular needle for Magic Loop technique, or two-three sizes smaller than gauge needle (smallest needle, for Hat rib)

US 6 (4mm) 24" or longer circular needle, or two sizes smaller than gauge needle (medium needle, for Cowl/Scarf rib)

NOTIONS

Yarn Needle
Stitch Markers (optional)
Cable Needle
Scrap Yarn for optional Provisional Cast On
Crochet Hook for optional Provisional Cast On
4 Buttons for Cowl

GAUGE

28 sts and 25 rows = 4" in Cable pattern with largest needle, lightly blocked

For pattern support, contact tetianaotruta@gmail.com

Kai Hat, Cowl, and Long Scarf

Notes:
Hat is worked in the round. Number of cast on stitches and repeats for hat 17.25" and 18.75" sizes are written in parentheses where different.

Cowl and Scarf are worked flat. Number of repeats for large cowl and long scarf are written in parentheses where different.

Chart A is worked in the round; read all rows from right to left as RS rows. Chart B is worked flat; read RS rows (odd numbers) from right to left; read WS rows (even numbers) from left to right.

Pattern repeats are outlined in red.

Left 1/3 Cable (1/3 LC): SL 1 st to CN and hold in front, K3, K1 from CN.
Right 1/3 Cable (1/3 RC): SL 3 sts to CN and hold in back, K1, K3 from CN.
Left 1/2 Cable (1/2 LC): SL 1 st to CN and hold in front, K2, K1 from CN.
Right 1/2 Cable (1/2 RC): SL 2 sts to CN and hold in back, K1, K2 from CN.
Left 1/1 Cable (1/1 LC): SL 1 st to CN and hold in front, K1, K1 from CN.
Right 1/1 Cable (1/1 RC): SL 1 sts to CN and hold in back, K1, K1 from CN.

Slip st with YO (SL1 YO)
With the working yarn in front, SL1 st and make YO; the slipped st and YO are counted as one st. K SL st with YO tog on the next rnd; or P SL st with YO tog on WS if working flat.

1x1 Rib (worked in the rnd over multiples of 2 sts)
Rnd 1: (K1, P1) around.
Rep Rnd 1 for pattern.

1x1 Rib with Slip st edges (worked flat over multiples of 2 sts plus 1 st)
Row 1: SL1 WYIB, (P1, K1) to end.
Row 2: SL1 WYIF, (K1, P1) to end.
Rep Rows 1-2 for pattern.

Hat Cable Pattern (worked in the rnd over multiples of 11 sts), Chart A
Rnd 1: 1/3 LC, 1/3 RC, P1, SL1 YO, P1.
Rnd 2: K8, P1, K1, P1.
Rep Rnds 1-2 for pattern.

Cowl/Scarf Cable Pattern (worked flat over multiples of 11 sts), Chart A
Row 1 (RS): 1/3 LC, 1/3 RC, P1, SL1 YO, P1.
Row 2 (WS): K1, P1, K1, P8.
Rep Rows 1-2 for pattern.

HAT DIRECTIONS

With largest needles CO 80 (88, 96) sts. Join sts in the rnd and PM for rnd beginning, being careful not to twist sts. With smallest needles work 10 rnds of 1x1 Rib in the rnd. Switch to largest needles.
Next Rnd (Inc): (K1, M1R, K1, KFB, K1, M1L, K1, P1, K1, P1) rep around. 110 (121, 132) sts.
Using chart or written instruction work Rnds 1-2 of Chart A 16 (18, 20) times. Then, work Rnd 1 once.

Crown Shaping

Rnd 1: *K1, SKP, K2, K2tog, K1, P1, K1, P1; rep from * around. 90 (99, 108) sts.
Rnd 2: *1/2 LC, 1/2 RC, P1, SL1 YO, P1; rep from * around.
Rnd 3: *K6, P1, K1, P1; rep from * around.
Rnds 4-6: Rep Rnds 2-3 one more time; then rep Rnd 2 once.
Rnd 7: *K1, SKP, K2tog, K1, P1, K1, P1; rep from * around. 70 (77, 84) sts.
Rnd 8: *1/1 LC, 1/1 RC, P1, SL1 YO, P1; rep from * around.
Rnd 9: *K4, P1, K1, P1; rep from * around.
Rnds 10-12: Rep Rnds 8-9 one more time; then rep Rnd 8 once.
Rnd 13: *SKP, K2tog, P1, K1, P1; rep from * around. 50 (55, 60) sts.
Rnd 14: *K2, P1, SL1 YO, P1; rep from * around.
Rnd 15: *K2tog, P1, K1, P1; rep from * around. 40 (44, 48) sts.
Rnd 16: SKP around. 20 (22, 24) sts.
Rnd 17: K2tog around. 10 (11, 12) sts.

Hat Finishing

Cut the yarn leaving an 6" tail. Draw the yarn tail through the remaining 10 (11, 12) sts with yarn needle and pull to close top of hat.

Weave in ends, and block your hat.

COWL AND SCARF DIRECTIONS

With scrap yarn and crochet hook, chain 50-55 sts.
Leaving about a 2 yards tail of the working yarn and with medium needles, PU and K 49 sts from the back loops of your crochet chain.
Note: You may omit the provisional CO and use the Long Tail CO method with larger needle if desired.
Continuing with medium needle, work 10 rows of 1x1 Rib with Slip st edges.
Switch to largest needle.
Inc Row (RS): SL1 WYIB, (P1, K1) twice, P1, (K1, M1R, K1, KFB, K1, M1L, K1, P1, SL1 YO, P1) four times, K1, M1R, K1, KFB, K1, M1L, K1, (P1, K1) three times. 64 sts.
Next Row (WS): SL1 WYIF, (K1, P1) twice, K1, (P8, K1, P1, K1) four times, P8, (K1, P1) three times.

Body

Begin Chart B, or follow written directions below.
Row 1 (RS): SL1 WYIB, (P1, K1) twice, P1, (1/3 LC, 1/3 RC, P1, SL1 YO, P1) four times, 1/3 LC, 1/3 RC, (P1, K1) three times.
Row 2 (WS): SL1 WYIF, (K1, P1) twice, K1, (P8, K1, P1, K1) four times, P8, (K1, P1) three times.

Rep Rows 1-2 until the piece measures 22.5 (42, 69.5)" from CO edge.
Switch to medium needle.
Dec Row (RS): SL1 WYIB, (P1, K1) twice, P1, (SKP, P1, K2tog, P1, K2tog, P1, K1, P1) four times, SKP, P1, K2tog, P1, K2tog, (P1, K1) three times. 49 sts.
Next Row (WS): SL1 WYIF, (K1, P1) to end.

For Small/Large Cowl:
Work 2 rows of 1x1 Rib with Slip st edges.
Buttonhole Row (RS): SL1 WYIB, (P1, K1) twice, *YO, K2tog, (P1, K1) five times; rep from * 3 times, P1, SKP, YO, (K1, P1) twice, K1.
Work five rows of 1x1 Rib with Slip st edges.

For Long Scarf: Work 8 rows of 1x1 Rib with Slip st edges.

Bind Off
Remove crochet chain from provisional CO edge and place resulting live sts on medium needle.
With larger needle, BO all sts P-wise on RS.

Cowl and Scarf Finishing

Weave in yarn ends, block lightly, and trim yarn ends after blocking. Large/Small Cowl: Attach buttons opposite buttonholes.

Kai Hat, Cowl, and Long Scarf

Chart A

11	10	9	8	7	6	5	4	3	2	1	ROW	RND
•	•										2	
•	⌀	•	\\\\	\\\\	\\\\	//	//	//			1	1

Chart B

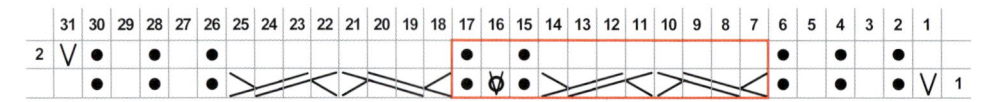

31	30	29	28	27	26	25	24	23	22	21	20	19	18	17	16	15	14	13	12	11	10	9	8	7	6	5	4	3	2	1	
V	•	•	•	•										•	•	•	•	•	•	•					•	•	•	•			2
	•	•	•	•	\\\\	\\\\	\\\\	//	//	//				•	⌀	•	\\\\	\\\\	\\\\	//	//	//			•	•	•	•		V	1

Legend:

□ **Knit**
RS: knit stitch
WS: purl stitch

• **Purl**
RS: purl stitch
WS: knit stitch

V **Slip**
RS: Slip stitch as if to purl, holding yarn in back
WS: Slip stitch as if to purl, holding yarn in front

□ **Pattern Repeat**

⌀ **SL1 YO**
With the working yarn in front, SL1 and make YO; the slipped st and YO are counted as one st.
Next row/rnd: either P SL with YO tog on WS if working flat, or K SL st with YO tog if working in the rnd

C1 Over 3 Right (1/3 RC)
SL3 to CN, hold in back.
K1, K3 from CN

C1 Over 3 Left (1/3 LC)
SL1 to CN, hold in front.
K3, K1 from CN

40 Kai Hat, Cowl, and Long Scarf

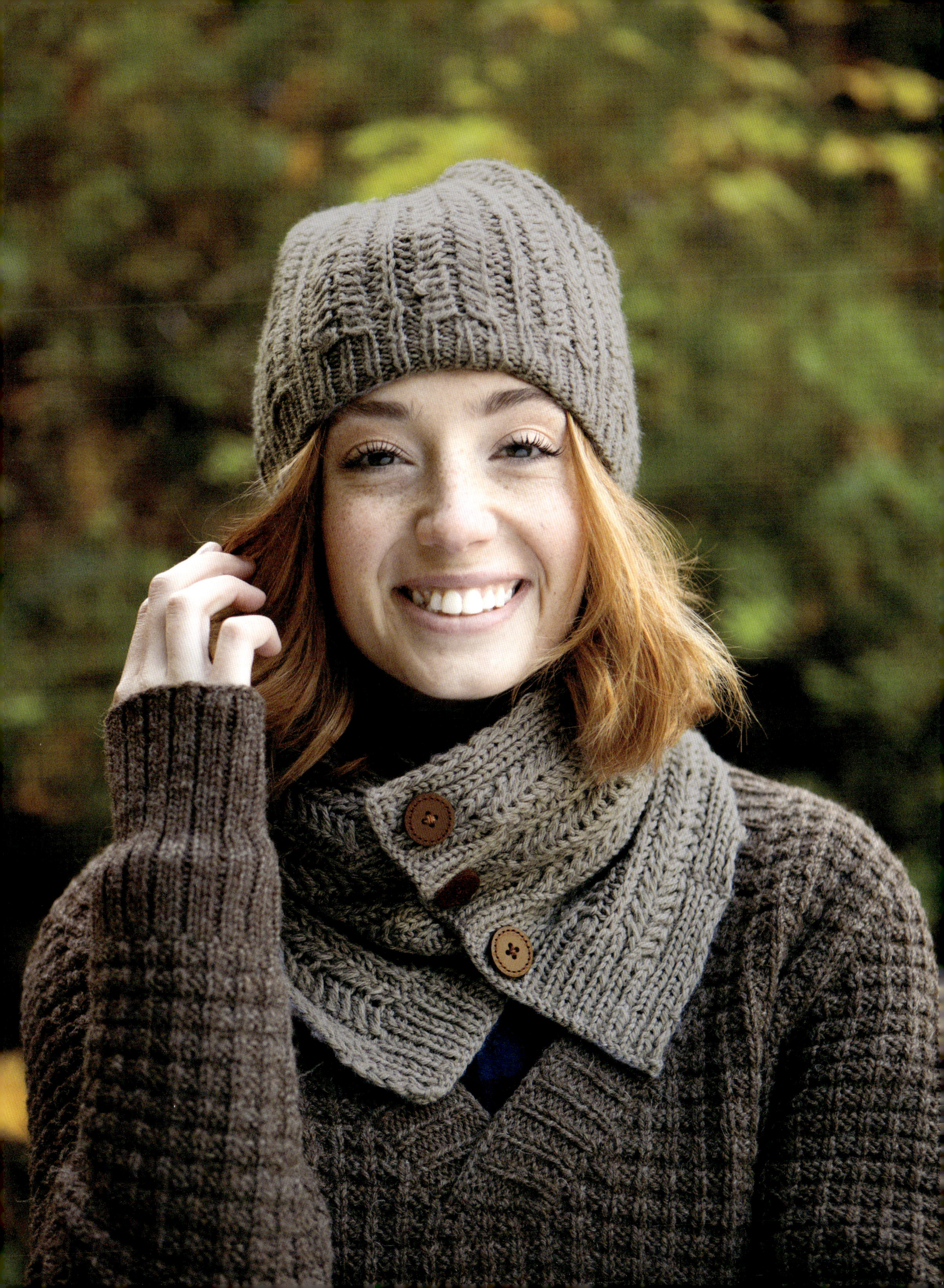

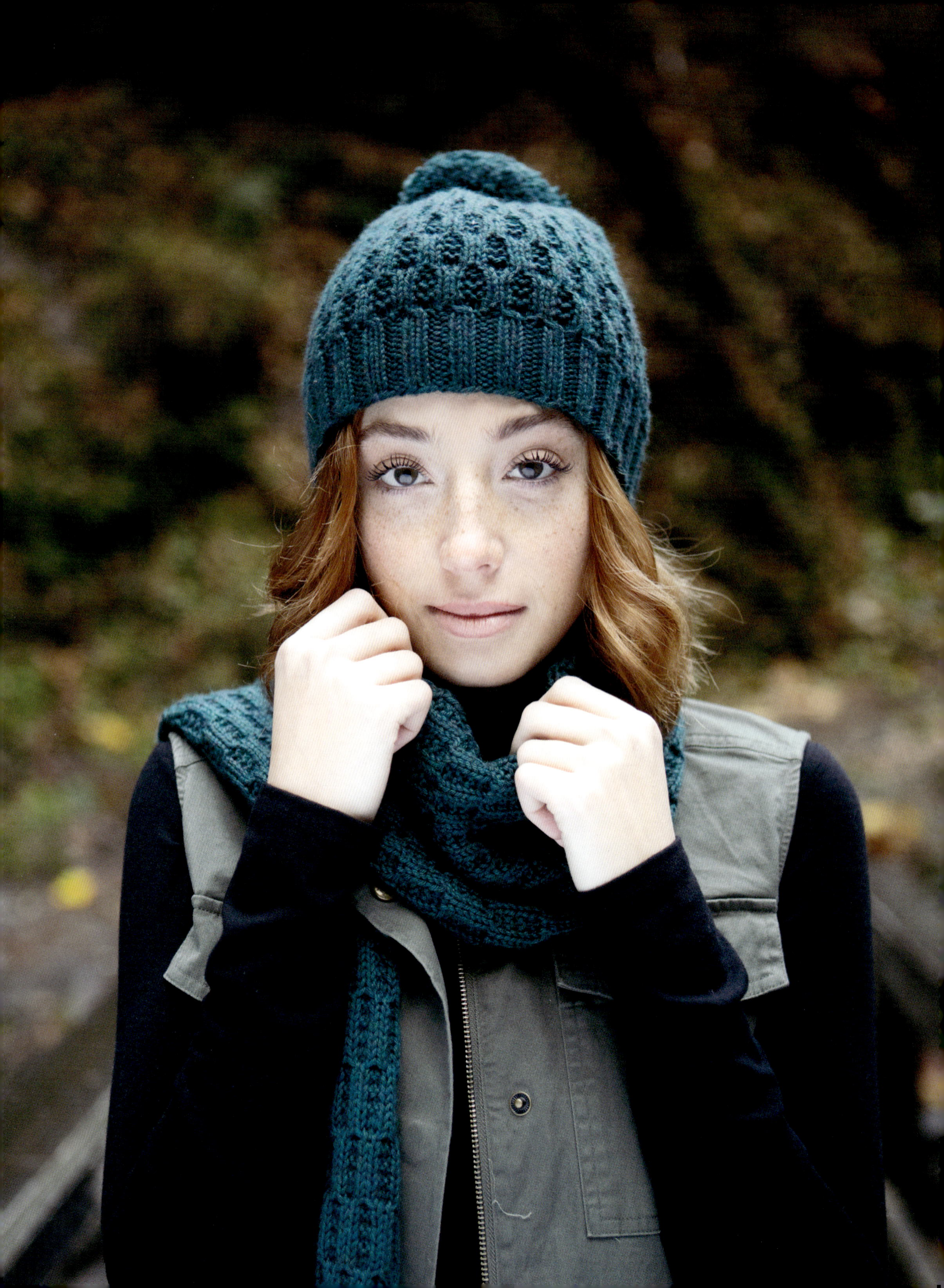

OGEE HAT AND SCARF

by Holli Yeoh

FINISHED MEASUREMENTS
Hat: 17.5 (19, 20.25)" circumference x 8.5 (10, 11)" height (not including pom-pom): hat is meant to be worn with 10-15% negative ease. Choose a finished size about 2-3.5" smaller than head.
Scarf: 8" x 60"

YARN
Knit Picks Swish (DK weight, 100% Fine Superwash Merino Wool; 123 yards/50g): Rainforest Heather 25585, 7 balls for set, Hat: 3 skeins, Scarf: 5 skeins

NEEDLES
Hat: US 6 (4mm) DPNs plus 16" circular needle, or two 24" circular needles for two circulars technique, or one 32" or longer circular needle for Magic Loop technique, or size to obtain gauge.
US 4 (3.5mm) 16" circular needle, or two 24" circular needles for two circulars technique, or one 32" or longer circular needle for Magic Loop technique, or 2 sizes smaller than needle used to obtain gauge.
Scarf: US 6 (4mm) straight or circular needles, or size to obtain gauge

NOTIONS
Yarn Needle
Stitch Markers
Cable Needle (optional)
Size H Crochet Hook (optional, for Scarf Fringe)
Large Pom-Pom Maker (optional)

GAUGE
Hat: 22 sts and 30.5 rnds = 4" in Ogee Rib in the round on larger needle, blocked
Scarf: 22 sts and 30.5 rows = 4" in Ogee Rib worked flat, blocked; 24 sts and 32 rows = 4" in Ogee Rib worked flat, before blocking

For pattern support, contact info@holliyeoh.com

Ogee Hat and Scarf

Notes:

Undulating ribbing flows over a field of garter stitch, with twisted stitches adding depth and texture as well as knitting interest. The fabric lies flat naturally, making a neat all-over scarf pattern and a cozy air-trapping hat.

A cheery fringe and just the right amount of slouch make these the wearable winter accessories you'll reach for every day.

The hat is worked from bottom up. Use your favorite method for knitting in the round: 16″ circular needle plus DPNs, two circular needles, or Magic Loop with one long circular needle. If using 16″ circular needle, change to DPNs when there are too few sts to fit comfortably on a circular needle.

All slip sts are worked P-wise, with yarn on WS.

When following a chart in the rnd, read all rows from right to left as RS rows. When working flat, read RS rows (odd numbers) from right to left, and WS rows (even numbers) from left to right.

I find simple cable crosses or in this case, twisted stitches, easier without a cable needle. Take this opportunity to try it out (instructions included). Optionally, a cable needle can be used as follows.
RT: SL 1 to CN, hold in back. K1, K1 from CN.
LT: SL 1 to CN, hold in front. K1, K1 from CN.

2x2 Rib (worked in the rnd over a multiple of 4 sts)
All Rnds: *K2, P2; rep from * to end of rnd.

Ogee Rib Round (worked in the rnd over a multiple of 4 sts)
Rnd 1: *LT, RT; rep from * to end of rnd.
Rnd 2: Knit all.
Rnd 3: *P1, K2, P1; rep from * to end of rnd.
Rnds 4-8: Rep Rnds 2-3, ending with a Rnd 2.
Rnd 9: *RT, LT; rep from * to end of rnd.
Rnd 10: Knit all.
Rnd 11: *K1, P2, K1; rep from * to end of rnd.
Rnds 12-16: Rep Rnds 10-11, ending with a Rnd 10.
Rep Rnds 1 to 16 for Ogee Rib Round pattern.

Ogee Rib Flat (worked flat over a multiple of 4 sts, plus 4)
Row 1 (RS): *RT, LT; rep from * to end of row.
Row 2 (WS): SL1 WYIF, P to end of row.
Row 3: SL1 WYIB, *P2, K2; rep from * to last 3 sts, P2, K1.
Rows 4-8: Rep Rows 2-3, ending with a Row 2.
Row 9: *LT, RT; rep from * to end of row.
Row 10: SL1 WYIF, P to end of row.
Row 11: SL1 WYIB, *K2, P2; rep from * to last 3 sts, K3.
Rows 12-16: Rep Rows 10-11, ending with a Row 10.
Rep Rows 1-16 for Ogee Rib Flat pattern.

RM: Remove marker.

Right Twist, without a Cable Needle (RT)
Insert right needle into front of second st on needle and knit it, leaving sts on left needle. Then knit first st on left needle, allowing both sts to drop off needle.

Left Twist, without a Cable Needle (LT)
Insert right needle into back of second st on needle and knit it TBL, leaving sts on left needle. Then knit first st on left needle, allowing both sts to drop off needle.

HAT DIRECTIONS

With smaller needle(s) and using Cable cast on, CO 96 (104, 112) sts.
PM for beginning of rnd and join, taking care not to twist sts.
Work in 2x2 Rib until piece measures 1.5 (2, 2)".

Begin Ogee Rib Round

Change to larger needle(s).
Beginning with Rnd 1, work Ogee Rib Round until hat measures approximately 6.25 (7.75, 8.75)" from CO, ending with Rnd 4 (12, 4) of pattern.

Shape Crown

Note: Change to DPNs when there are too few sts to fit comfortably on a circular needle.

Sizes 17.5, 20.25" Only

Occasionally, end of rnd marker is moved over by one st. When that happens, the marker indicates the new end of rnd.
Dec Rnd 1: RM, SL1, PM, *K2, P2tog; rep from * to end of rnd. 72 (–, 84) sts.
Rnd 2: Knit all.
Rnd 3: *K2, P1; rep from * to end of rnd.
Dec Rnd 4: RM, SL1, PM, *K1, K2tog; rep from * to end of rnd. 48 (–, 56) sts.

Size 19" Only

Dec Rnd 1: *K1, P2tog, K1; rep from * to end of rnd. – (78, –) sts.
Rnd 2: Knit all.
Rnd 3: *K1, P1, K1; rep from * to end of rnd.
Dec Rnd 4: *K1, K2tog; rep from * to end of rnd. – (52, –) sts.

All Sizes

Rnd 5: *RT, LT; rep from * to M.
Rnd 6 and even numbered rnds: Knit all.
Rnd 7: *K1, P2, K1; rep from * to end of rnd.
Dec Rnd 9: *K1, P2tog, K1; rep from * to M. 36 (39, 42) sts.
Rnd 11: *K1, P1, K1; rep from * to end of rnd.
Dec Rnd 12: *K1, K2tog; rep from * to M. 24 (26, 28) sts.
Rnd 13: Knit all.
Dec Rnd 14: K2tog to end of rnd. 12 (13, 14) sts.
Cut yarn leaving an 8" tail and thread through remaining sts. Pull tightly and secure end.

Hat Finishing

Weave in ends, wash, and block to dimensions.

Pom-Pom (optional)

Make a 4" pom-pom and secure to top of hat.

SCARF DIRECTIONS

With larger needles CO 44 sts.
Row 1 (RS): SL1, *K2, P2; rep from * to last 3 sts, K3.
Row 2 (WS): SL1, P to end.
Rep Rows 1-2 three more times, ending with a WS row.

Begin Ogee Rib Flat

Work 16-row rep 28 times. Scarf measures approximately 57" from beginning.
Work Rows 1-14 once more.
BO all sts.

Scarf Finishing

Weave in ends, wash, and block to finished measurements.

Fringe (optional)

Cut 110 pieces of yarn, each 13" in length. Hold 5 strands together and fold in half. With crochet hook inserted from WS to RS through base of K2 element of st pattern on CO edge, draw looped end of fringe part way though scarf. Pass cut ends through loop and tighten to secure. Attach fringe at base of each K2 element of st pattern until there are 11 evenly spaced along edge. Rep along BO edge.
Trim, if needed, to even ends.

Legend:

☐ **Knit**
RS: knit stitch
WS: purl stitch

• **Purl**
RS: purl stitch
WS: knit stitch

V **Slip**
RS: Slip stitch as if to purl, holding yarn in back
WS: Slip stitch as if to purl, holding yarn in front

⧖ **Right Twist**
SL1 to CN, hold in back, K1, K1 from CN

⧗ **Left Twist**
SL1 to CN, hold in front, K1, K1 from CN

Ogee Round

4	3	2	1	
				16
	•	•		15
				14
	•	•		13
				12
	•	•		11
				10
⧗	⧖	⧗	⧖	9
				8
•			•	7
				6
•			•	5
				4
•			•	3
				2
⧖	⧗	⧖	⧗	1

Ogee Flat

8	7	6	5	4	3	2	1	
16 V							V	16/15
		•	•				V	15
14 V							V	14/13
		•	•				V	13
12 V							V	12/11
		•	•				V	11
10 V							V	10
⧗	⧖	⧗	⧖	⧗	⧖	⧗	⧖	9
8 V							V	8
		•	•		•	•	V	7
6 V							V	6
		•	•		•	•	V	5
4 V							V	4
		•	•		•	•	V	3
2 V							V	2
⧖	⧗	⧖	⧗	⧖	⧗	⧖	⧗	1

46 Ogee Hat and Scarf

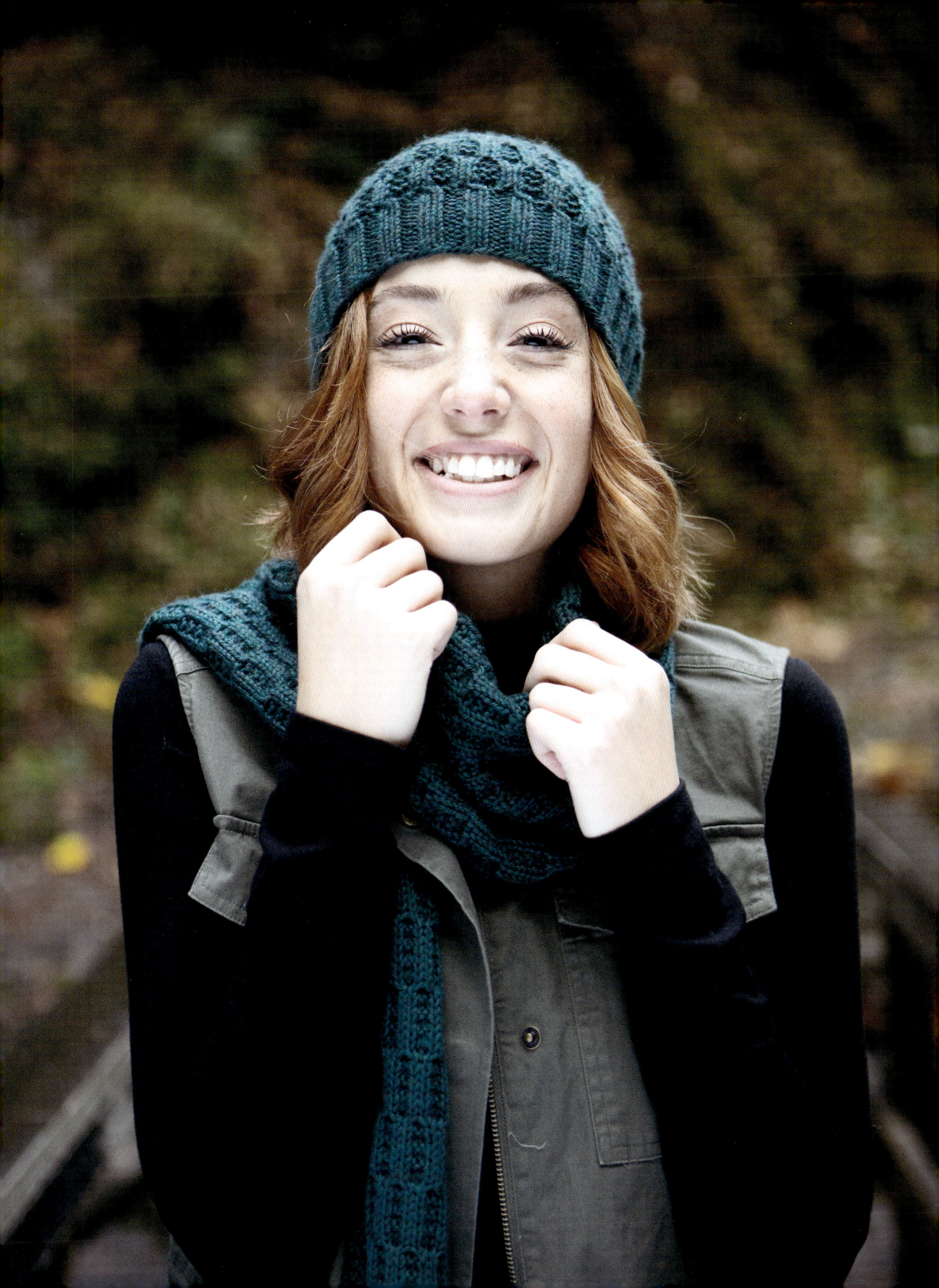

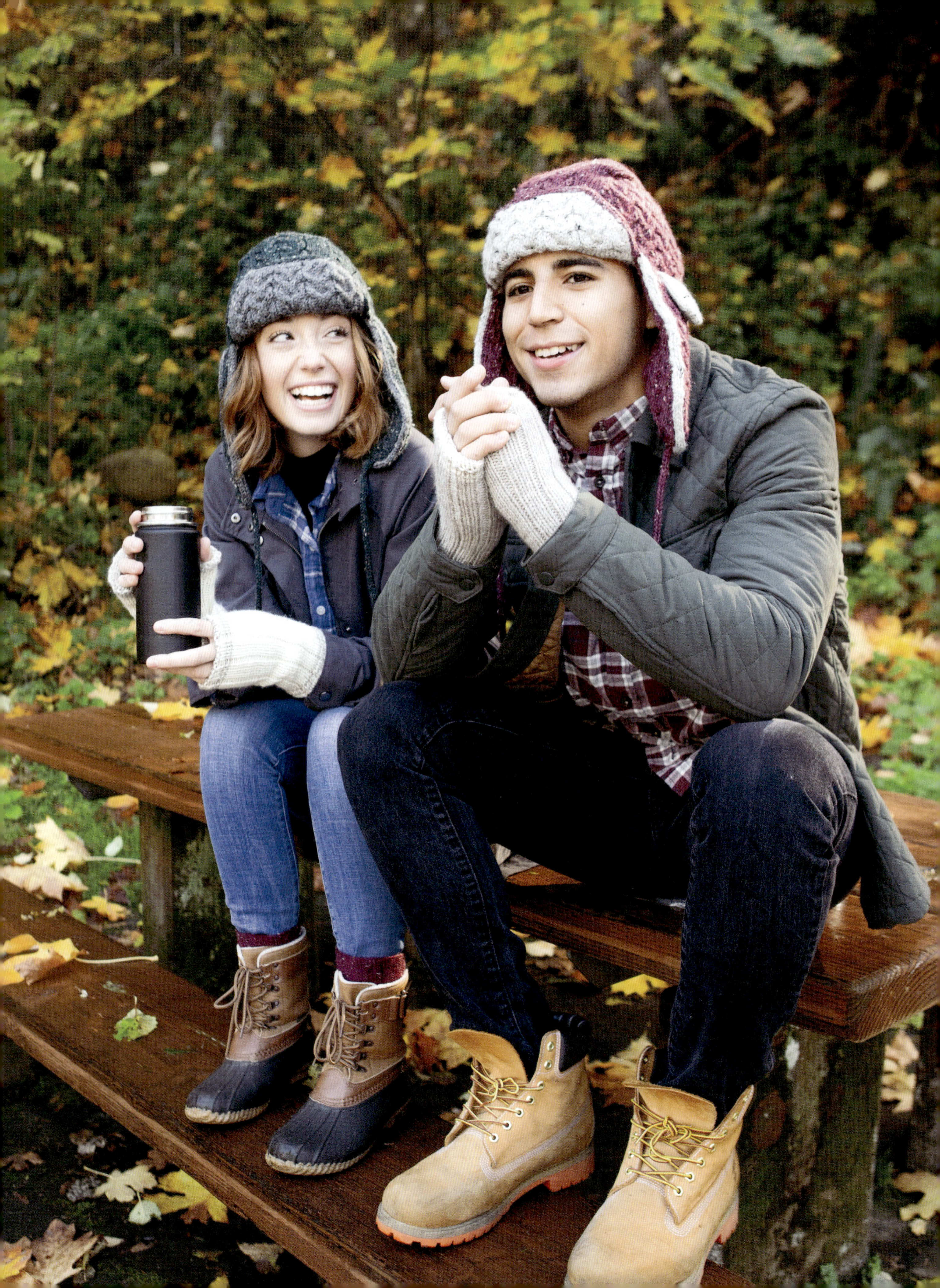

ORIEL

by Maria Leigh

FINISHED MEASUREMENT
S (M, L) to fit 21-22.5 (22.5-24, 24- 26)" head circumference; hat is meant to be worn with 0.75 to 1.5" ease

YARN
Knit Picks Wool of the Andes Tweed (worsted weight, 80% Peruvian Highland Wool, 20% Donegal Tweed; 110 yards/ 50g):
Option 1: MC Sequoia Heather 25448, 3 (4, 4) skeins; C1 Flagstone 25457, 2 (2, 2) skeins
Option 2: MC Barn Door Heather 25454, 3 (4, 4) skeins; C1 Down Heather 25458, 2 (2, 2) skeins

NEEDLES
US 6 (4mm) DPNs and 16" circular needles, 32" circular needles if using Magic Loop, or size to obtain gauge
US 5 (3.75mm) DPNs and 16" circular needle, 32" circular needles if using Magic Loop, or one size smaller than size to obtain gauge

NOTIONS
Yarn Needle
Stitch Markers
Stitch Holder or Spare Needle
Cable Needle

GAUGE
24 sts and 30 rows = 4" in stockinette stitch in the round on larger needles, blocked
28 sts and 30 rows = 4" over FB Panel Chart pattern in the round on larger needles, blocked

For pattern support, contact amigurumikr@gmail.com

Oriel

Notes:
Oriel was inspired by a traditional Siberian trapper hat. This kind of double layer hat is the same as making two different hats separately. Make the outer hat first, and then make the inner hat. It is joined through two processes; whip stitch on the cast on edge, and a unique edging that uses a combination of 3-Needle Bind Off and Applied I-Cord.

When working a chart in the rnd, read all rows from right to left as RS rows. When working flat, read RS rows from right to left, and WS rows from left to right.

2/2 LC: SL 2 sts to CN, hold in front; K2, K2 from CN.
2/2 RC: SL 2 sts to CN, hold in back; K2, K2 from CN.

FB: Front and Back.

DIRECTIONS
Outer Hat: Crown
Using MC and larger needle, CO 122 (130, 138) sts. Join in the rnd being careful not to twist, PM.
Setup Rnd 1: K all.
Setup Rnd 2: *K1 (3, 5), KFB, (KFB, K5, KFB) twice, K1 (3, 5), KFB, K3, KFB, (KFB, K5, KFB) 5 times, K3, KFB; rep from * twice. 158 (166, 174) sts.
Setup Rnd 3: *K1, PM, K1 (3, 5), P1, (K8, P1) twice, K1 (3, 5), PM, K1, P1, K4, P1, (K8, P1) 5 times, K4, P1; rep from * twice. Then K1 next st.
There are 58 sts for each side panel, 21 (25, 29) sts for each FB panel. 158 (166, 174) sts.

Rnds 1-32, begin Charts: (FB Panel Chart, Side Panel Chart) twice. There are 28 sts for each side panel and 25 (29, 33) sts for FB panel after Rnd 32.
Begin to work back and forth. At the end of RS rows, work charted SSK as last st of FB panel with first st of next Side panel, then turn work. At the end of WS rows, work charted P2tog as last st of FB panel with first st of next Side panel, then turn. Work FB Panel Chart Rows 33-58. 24 (28, 32) sts remain for back panel.
Break yarn and remove M. Place remaining sts on holder or spare needle.
Place 13 sts of Side panel onto RH needle on RS. Join a new yarn. Cont to work back and forth, rep Rows 33-58 once more for front panel. 24 (28, 32) sts.
Break yarn and remove M.
Graft Front and Back panels together on RS, using Kitchener St.

Outer Hat: Mini Flap (make 2 - optional)
Using C1 and larger needle, CO 18 sts. Divide 9 sts each on two DPNs alternately by holding two DPNs parallel on RH, *SL 1 st onto needle closest to you, then SL next st onto needle furthest away to you; rep from * 9 times. 9 sts on front needle, 9 sts on back needle. Join to work in the rnd, being careful not to twist.
PM and Knit 1 rnd.
Next Rnd: (K1, M1R, K7, M1L, K1) twice. 22 sts.
Next Rnd: K all.
Next Rnd: (K1, M1R, K9, M1L, K1) twice. 26 sts.
Knit around until piece measures 2" from CO edge. 26 sts total; 13 sts on each needle.
Break yarn and set aside to work together with Flap.

Outer Hat: Flap
Leave 38 (42, 46) of center CO sts on Outer Crown. Using MC and larger needle, PU and K 5 sts on CO edge, place mini flap on the CO edge, PU and K 13 sts through a single st from each needle of mini flap and CO edge, PU 48 (52, 56) sts on CO edge, PU 13 sts through a single st from each needle of mini flap and CO edge once more, PU and K 5 sts. 84 (88, 92) sts.

Size S Only
Setup Row 1 (WS): P across.
Setup Row 2 (RS): K1, KFB, (K1, KFB, K4, KFB) 4 times, K4, P1, (K1, KFB, K4, KFB) twice, K4, P1, (K1, KFB, K4, KFB) 4 times, K2. 105 sts.
Setup Row 3: P2, (K1, P8) 4 times, K1, P4, (K1, P8) 2 times, K1, P4, (K1, P8) 4 times, K1, P2.

Size M Only
Setup Row 1 (WS): P across.
Setup Row 2 (RS): K1, KFB, (K1, KFB, K4, KFB) 12 times, K2. 113 sts.
Setup Row 3: P2, (K1, P8) 12 times, K1, P2.

Size L Only
Setup Row 1 (WS): P across.
Setup Row 2 (RS): K1, KFB, (K1, KFB, K4, KFB) 5 times, K1, P1, (K1, KFB, K4, KFB) twice, K1, P1, (K1, KFB, K4, KFB) 5 times, K2. 117 sts.
Setup Row 3: P2, (K1, P8) 5 times, K1, P1, (K1, P8) twice, K1, P1, (K1, P8) 5 times, K1, P2.

All Sizes
Work Flap Chart Rows 1-17.
BO 17 (27, 31) center sts on Row 18. Work each side of Flap separately over Rows 19-52.
BO remaining sts.

Outer Hat: Brim
Using C1 and smaller needle, PU and K38 (42, 46) sts on the center of CO edge.
Work in St st for Rows 1-10.
Row 11 (RS): SSK, K10 (11, 12), SSK, K10 (12, 14), K2tog, K10 (11, 12), K2tog. 4 sts dec.
Rows 12, 14, 16 (WS): P across.
Row 13: SSK, K8 (10, 11), SSK, K10 (10, 12), K2tog, K8 (10, 11), K2tog. 4 sts dec.
Row 15: SSK, K7 (9, 10), SSK, K8 (8, 10), K2tog, K7 (9, 10), K2tog. 4 sts dec.
Row 17: SSK, K6 (8, 9), SSK, K6 (6, 8), K2tog, K6 (K8, 9), K2tog. 4 sts dec.
Row 18: P2tog, P to last 2 sts, SSP. 2 sts dec.

Row 19: SSK, K to last 2 sts, K2tog. 2 sts dec.
Row 20: P2tog, P to last 2 sts, SSP. 2 sts dec. 16 (20, 24) sts.
BO remaining sts.

Inner Hat: Crown
Using C1 and smaller needle, CO 122 (130, 138) sts. Join in the rnd being careful not to twist.
Setup Rnd 1: K around, then K1.
Rnd 1: *K16 (20, 24), PM, K45, PM; rep from * twice.
Knit 15 (15, 13) rnds.
Dec Rnd: *K to M, SM, K2tog, K to 2 sts before M, SSK, SM; rep from * twice. 4 sts dec.
Rep Dec Rnd every other rnd 7 (7, 8) more times. End with Rnd 32. 90 (98, 102) sts.

Begin to work back and forth on the front and back, separately.
Row 1 (RS): K to M, SM, SSK, turn. 1 st dec.
Row 2 (WS): SL1, SM, P to M, SM, P2tog, turn. 1 st dec.
Row 3: SL1, SM, K to M, SM, SSK, turn. 1 st dec.
Rep Rows 2-3 12 more times, end with a RS row.
Remove 2 Ms and break yarn. Place remaining sts from just worked section on holder or spare needle.
Join a new yarn at the first M on RS.
Row 1 (RS): SL1, K to M, SM, SSK, turn. 1 st dec.
Row 2 (WS): SL1, SM, P to M, SM, P2tog, turn. 1 st dec.
Rep Rows 1-2 12 more times, then RS Row 1 once more.
Remove Ms and break yarn.
Graft each Front and Back panels on RS together, using Kitchener St.

Inner Hat: Flap
Work Inner Flap the same as Outer Flap, without attaching Mini flaps.
Leave 38 (42, 46) center CO sts on Inner Crown. Using MC and larger needle, PU and K 84 (88, 92) sts.

Size S Only
Setup Row 1 (WS): P across.
Setup Row 2 (RS): K1, KFB, (K1, KFB, K4, KFB) 4 times, K4, P1, (K1, KFB, K4, KFB) twice, K4, P1, (K1, KFB, K4, KFB) 4 times, K2. 103 sts.
Setup Row 3: P2, (K1, P8) 4 times, K1, P4, (K1, P8) 2 times, K1, P4, (K1, P8) 4 times, K1, P2.

Size M Only
Setup Row 1 (WS): P across.
Setup Row 2 (RS): K1, KFB, (K1, KFB, K4, KFB) 12 times, K2. 113 sts.
Setup Row 3: P2, (K1, P8) 12 times, K1, P2.

Size L Only
Setup Row 1 (WS): P across.
Setup Row 2 (RS): K1, KFB, (K1, KFB, K4, KFB) 5 times, K1, P1, (K1, KFB, K4, KFB) twice, K1, P1, (K1, KFB, K4, KFB) 5 times, K2. 117 sts.
Setup Row 3: P2, (K1, P8) 5 times, K1, P1, (K1, P8) twice, K1, P1, (K1, P8) 5 times, K1, P2.

All Sizes
Work Flap Chart Rows 1–17.
BO 17 (27, 31) center sts on Row 18.
Working each side separately, work Flap Rows 19–52.
BO remaining 15 sts.

I-Cord Ties (make 2 the same)
Using MC with smaller DPNs, PU and K 4 sts on BO edge of each Inner Flap as follows: There are 14 chains on the Flap edge. With RS facing, PU 4 sts only from front chains in the center. Leave back chains for Finishing.
Slide 4 sts to end of RH side of needle, K1, K2tog, K1. 1 st dec, ready to work a 3 st I-cord.
*Slide 3 sts to end of RH side of needle, K3; rep from * until it measures 10", and BO.

Inner Hat: Brim
Using C1 and larger needle, PU and K 39 (43, 47) sts on RS CO edge.
Setup Row 1 (WS): P across.
Setup Row 2 (RS): K1 (3, 5), KFB, (KFB, K5, KFB) 5 times, K2 (4, 6). 50 (54, 58) sts.
Setup Row 3: P2 (4, 6), (K1, P8) 5 times, K1, P2 (4, 6).
Work Brim Chart Rows 1–20 back and forth.
BO all sts loosely.

Finishing
Block lightly before joining Inner and Outer hat.

Joining Inner and Outer Hat
With WS facing each other, Whip st sts on CO edge.

Using C1 and smaller needle, PU and K sts, st by st and row by row, around. PU sts starting from right corner of Outer flap around Outer hat edge on outside facing. Turn inside out and prepare another smaller needle. PU same numbers of sts st by st and row by row around Inner hat edge from right side corner of Inner Brim. Turn hat once more, outside facing.

Work attached I-cord as follows: Holding the 2 needles together as if to work 3-Needle Bind Off, CO 3 sts onto front needle using Backward Loop method, *K2, SL1, put RH needle tip through first st of each needle, K2tog (like 3-Needle Bind Off), pass slipped st over it, SL the 3 worked sts from right needle to left front needle; rep from * around flap and then switch to MC, and cont repeating around Brim. Graft remaining 3 sts onto CO edge.

Weave in yarn tails, and block lightly.

Legend:

- ☐ **Knit**
  RS: knit stitch
  WS: purl stitch

- • **Purl**
  RS: purl stitch
  WS: knit stitch

- ■ **No Stitch**
  Placeholder—no stitch made

- M **Make One**
  Make one by lifting strand in between the stitch just worked and the next stitch, knit into the back of this thread

- ╱ **K2tog**
  RS: Knit two stitches together as one stitch
  WS: Purl two stitches together as one stitch

- ╲ **SSK**
  RS: Slip one stitch as if to knit, slip another stitch as if to knit. Insert left-hand needle into front of these 2 stitches and knit them together
  WS: Slip one stitch as if to purl, slip another stitch as if to purl. Slip these stitches back to the left-hand needle and purl stitches together through the back loop

- ◢ **Bind Off**

- **C2 Over 2 Right (2/2 RC)**
  SL 2 to CN, hold in back. K2, K2 from CN

- **C2 Over 2 Left (2/2 LC)**
  SL 2 to CN, hold in front. K2, K2 from CN

- ■ Size M & L Only

- ■ Size L Only

*Please Note:
FB Panel Chart is worked in the round until round 33, then worked flat.

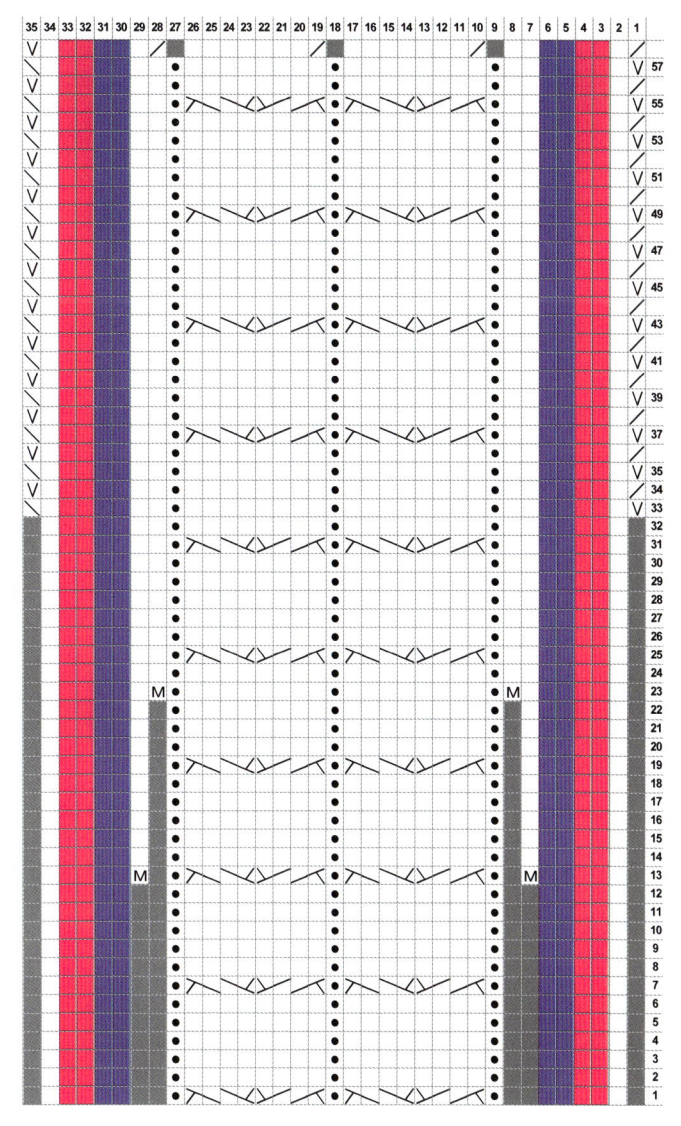

FB Panel Chart

Side Panel Chart

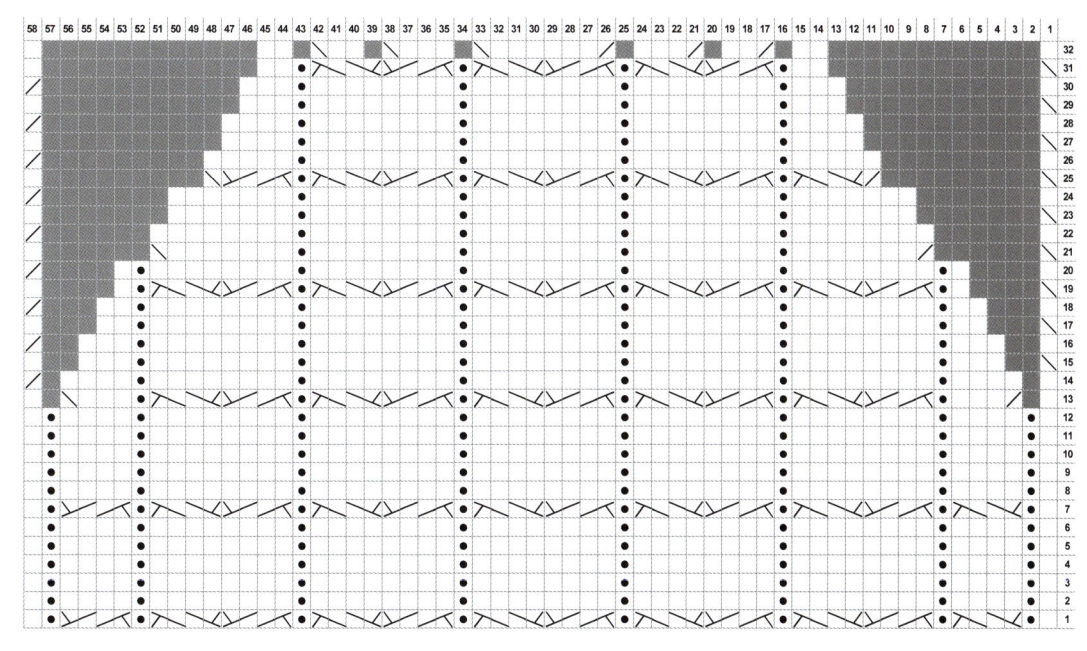

Oriel 53

Flap Chart

Brim Chart S

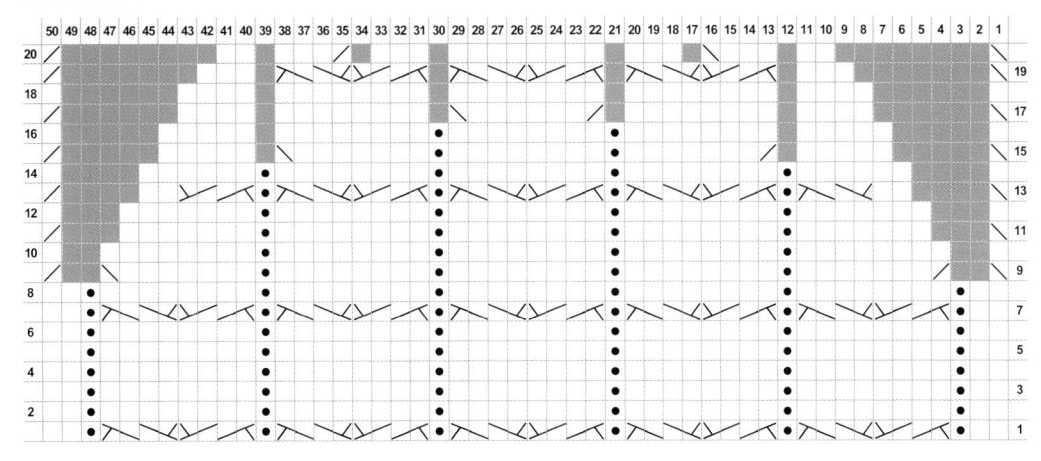

Brim Chart M

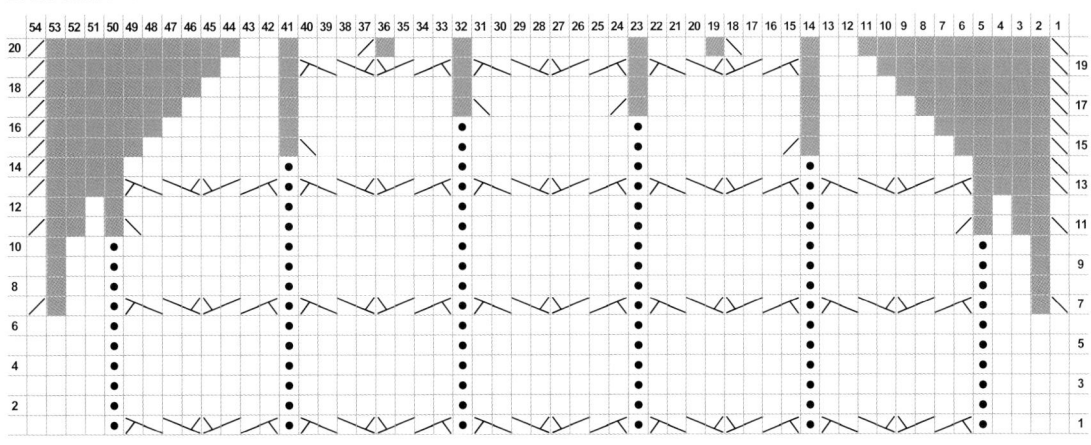

Brim Chart L

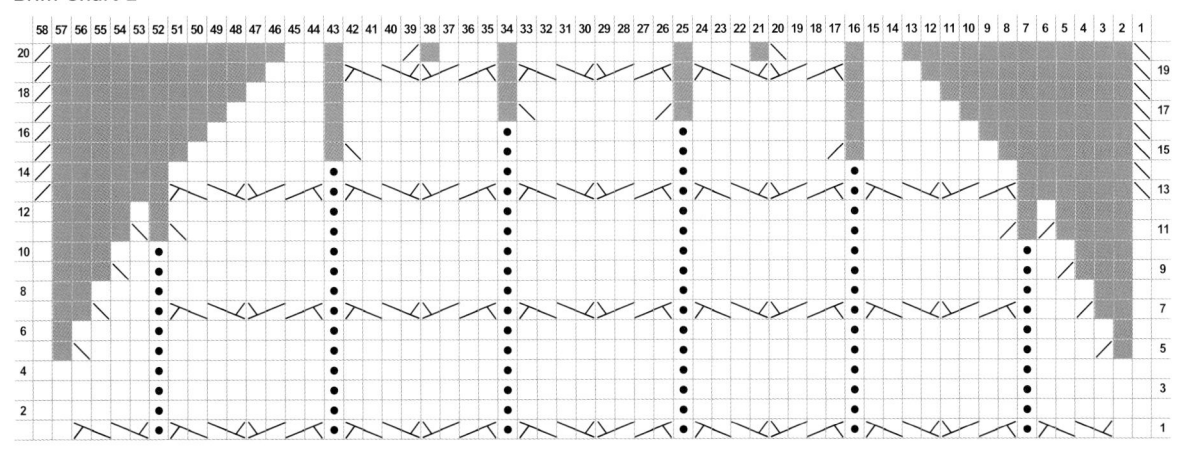

Oriel

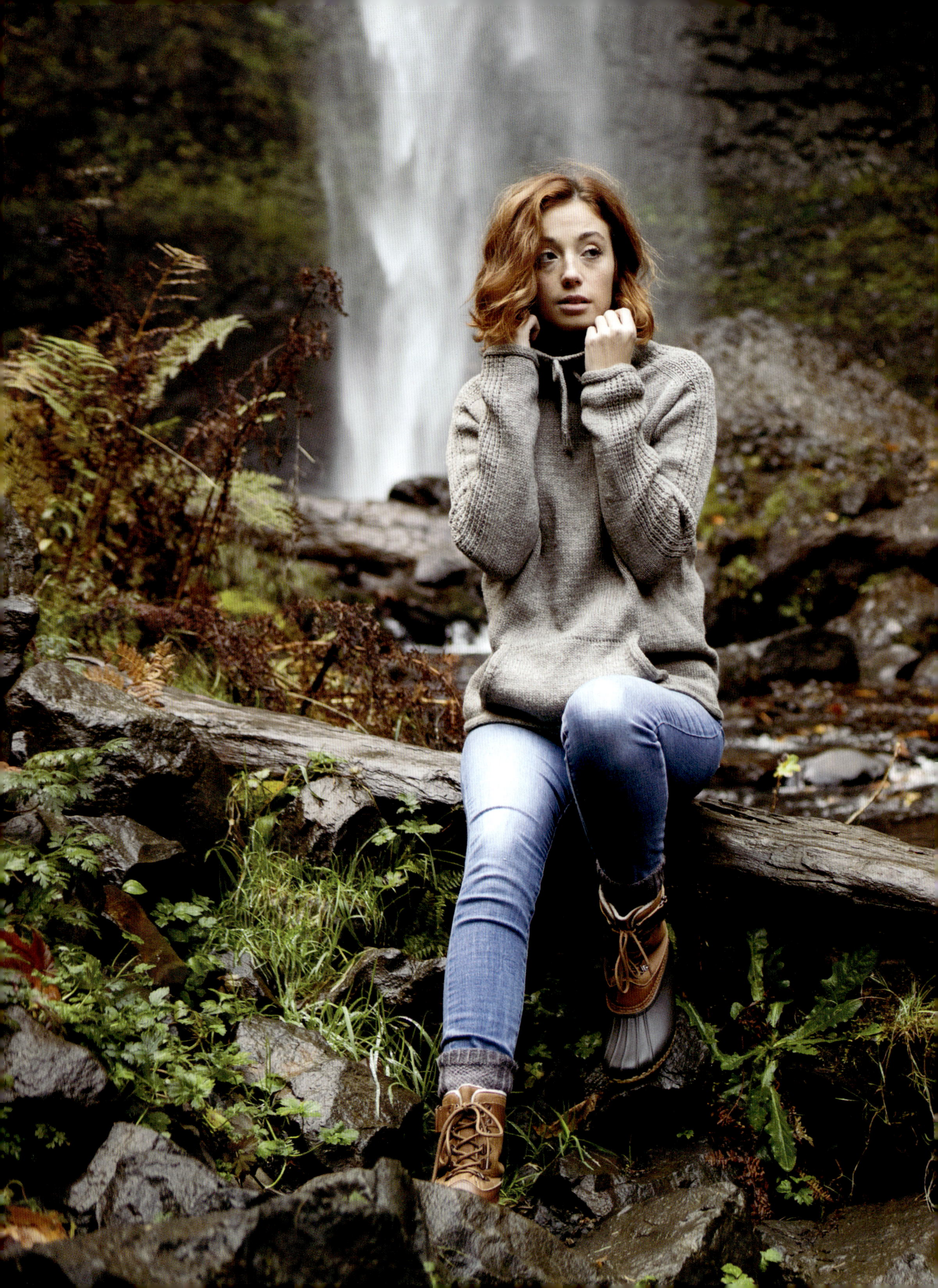

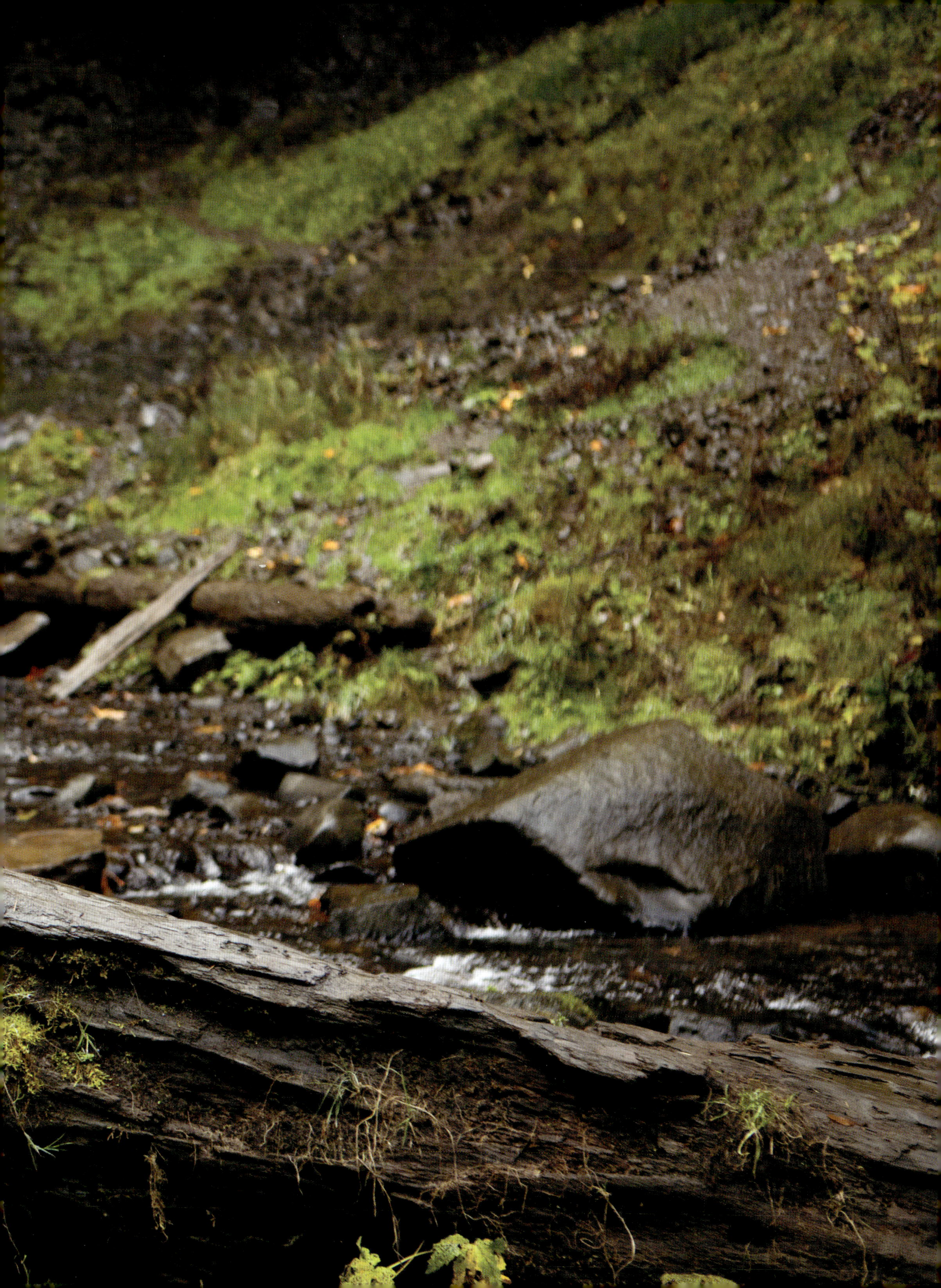

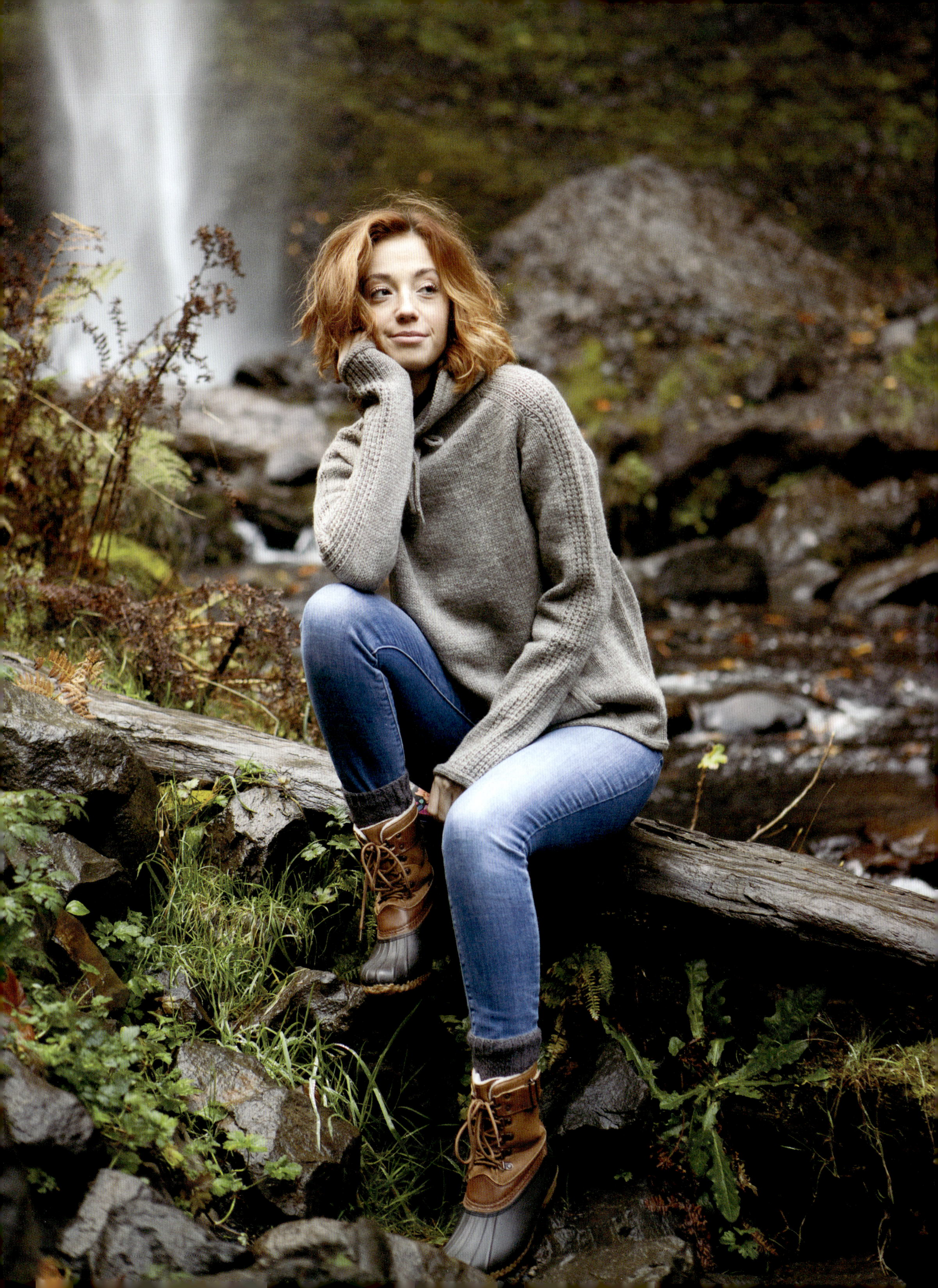

SLADE PULLOVER

by Cheryl Toy

FINISHED MEASUREMENTS
42 (46.5, 50, 54, 58, 62)" finished bust/chest measurement; garment is meant to be worn with 10" of positive ease

YARN
Knit Picks Simply Wool (worsted weight, 100% Eco Wool; 219 yards/100g): Wilbur 27474, 7 (7, 8, 8, 9, 10) hanks

NEEDLES
US 7 (4.5mm) DPNs, 16" and 40" circular needles, or size to obtain gauge

NOTIONS
Yarn Needle
Stitch Markers
Removable Stitch Markers
Stitch Holders
Scrap Yarn
Large Safety Pin

GAUGE
20 sts and 28 rows = 4" in stockinette stitch and seeded rib stitch in the round, blocked

For pattern support, contact cheryl@littlechurchknits.com

Slade Pullover

Notes:

This pullover is worked in the round from the top down using raglan shaping. Sleeves are worked from the top down and feature a seeded rib panel. Pocket is knitted into sweater front. Funnel neck is worked upward from neck stitches and finishes with a turned casing and I-cord drawstring. Sleeves and hem are edged in I-cord.

Super warm and capacious, the Slade Pullover is the voice in the wilderness for both women and men. Its lines are utterly clean and square but with a sophisticated saddle shoulder that showcases a minimalist panel of seeded rib patterning. Its deep funnel neck can be drawn up close around the neck for extra warmth, while a kangaroo pocket with slanted inserts waits ready to warm chilled hands. This no-nonsense unisex pullover is edged all around with I-cord.

Seeded Rib Stitch (in the rnd over an odd number of sts)
Rnd 1: *K1, P1; rep from * to last st, end P1.
Rnd 2: Knit all.
Rep Rnds 1-2 for pattern.

Make 1 Right (M1R)
With left needle, lift strand between needles from back to front, K TFL.

Make 1 Left (M1L)
With left needle, PU running thread between the last 2 sts from front to back, K TBL.

I-Cord Bind Off
With DPNs, CO 5 sts. Without turning needle, slide the sts to other end of needle. *Pull yarn snugly across the back of work, K4, Sl 1 P-wise to left needle holding live sts, K2tog TBL; rep from * until all sts have been bound off.

I-Cord
With DPN, CO 3 sts. *Without turning work, slide the sts to other end of needle, pull the yarn snugly across the back of work, K3; rep from * until cord reaches desired length.

DIRECTIONS

Yoke

With shorter circular and Long Tail method, CO 120 (122, 128, 132, 132, 132) sts, PM for beginning of rnd and join in the rnd, being careful not to twist sts.
Setup Rnd: *Work 15 (15, 15, 17, 17, 17) sts in Seeded Rib Stitch, PM, K45 (46, 49, 49, 49, 49), PM; rep from * once more.
Shoulder Inc Rnd: *Work in Seeded Rib Stitch to next M, SM, K2, M1L, K to 2 sts before next M, M1R, K2, SM; rep from * once more. 4 sts inc.
Work Shoulder Inc Rnd every rnd 14 (18, 18, 21, 23, 26) more times switching to longer circular when needed. 75 (84, 87, 93, 97, 103) sts each front and back. 180 (198, 204, 220, 228, 240) sts total.
Next Rnd: *M1L, work 15 (15, 15, 17, 17, 17) sts in Seeded Rib Stitch, M1R, SM, K to next M, SM; rep from * once more. 4 sts inc.

60 Slade Pullover

Sleeve Inc Rnd: *M1L, K to Seeded Rib panel, work Seeded Rib panel over next 15 (15, 15, 17, 17, 17) sts, K to next M, M1R, SM, K to next M, SM; rep from * once more. 4 sts inc.
Keeping to Seeded Rib Stitch over center 15 (15, 15, 17, 17, 17) sts as established and working new sts as St st, work Sleeve Inc Rnd every rnd 26 (26, 27, 31, 33, 37) more times. 71 (71, 73, 83, 87, 95) sts each sleeve. 292 (310, 320, 352, 368, 396) sts total.

Underarm Inc Rnd: *Work in pattern to next M, SM, K2, M1L, K to 2 sts before next M, M1R, K2, SM; rep from * once more. 4 sts inc.
Work Underarm Inc Rnd every rnd 14 (15, 18, 20, 23, 25) more times. 105 (116, 125, 135, 145, 155) sts each front and back, 71 (71, 73, 83, 87, 95) sts each sleeve. 352 (374, 396, 436, 464, 500) sts total.

Divide for Body and Sleeves

K71 (71, 73, 83, 87, 95), place these last 71 (71, 73, 83, 87, 95) sts on hold for left sleeve, K to next M, K71 (71, 73, 83, 87, 95), place these last 71 (71, 73, 83, 87, 95) sts on hold for right sleeve, K to end. 210 (232, 250, 270, 290, 310) sts remain.

Body

Work even in St st until piece measures 8 (8, 8.5, 8.5, 9, 10)" from underarm, or 7.5 (7.5, 7.5, 8, 8, 8)" shorter than desired body length.
Next Rnd: K33 (38, 42, 45, 48, 53), place removable M for pocket placement, K39, (40, 41, 49, 49, 49), using yarn needle, thread 24" of scrap yarn through these last 39, (40, 41, 49, 49, 49) sts, place removable M for pocket placement. WE in St st to 6 (6, 6, 7, 7, 7)" from scrap yarn. Body sts will remain on hold while pocket is worked.

Pocket (worked flat)

With shorter circular, PU K39, (40, 41, 49, 49, 49) sts held on scrap yarn for pocket. Join yarn at upper right corner of pocket, K to end. Remove scrap yarn.
Next Row (WS): Purl across.
Pocket Inc Row (RS): K1, M1R, K to 1 st before end, M1L, K1. 2 sts inc.
Work in St st, repeating Pocket Inc Row every 4th row 9 (9, 9, 10, 10, 10) more times. Place these 59 (60, 61, 71, 71, 71) sts on hold.

Return to body sts, K 23 (28, 32, 32, 37, 42) sts, place next 59 (60, 61, 71, 71, 71) body sts on hold for pocket lining, work across sts held for pocket, K to end of rnd.
Work body and pocket sts in the rnd for 1" in St st.
Return 59 (60, 61, 71, 71, 71) sts held for pocket lining to needle.
Work pocket lining sts flat for 1" in St st.

Return to body sts, working in the rnd.
Next Rnd: K23 (28, 32, 32, 37, 42) sts, *K1 st from body tog with 1 st from pocket lining; rep from * 58 (59, 60, 70, 70, 70) more times until all pocket lining sts are joined to body sts, K to end. 210 (232, 250, 270, 290, 310) sts.
Stitch short ends of pocket lining to body.
BO using I-Cord Bind Off.

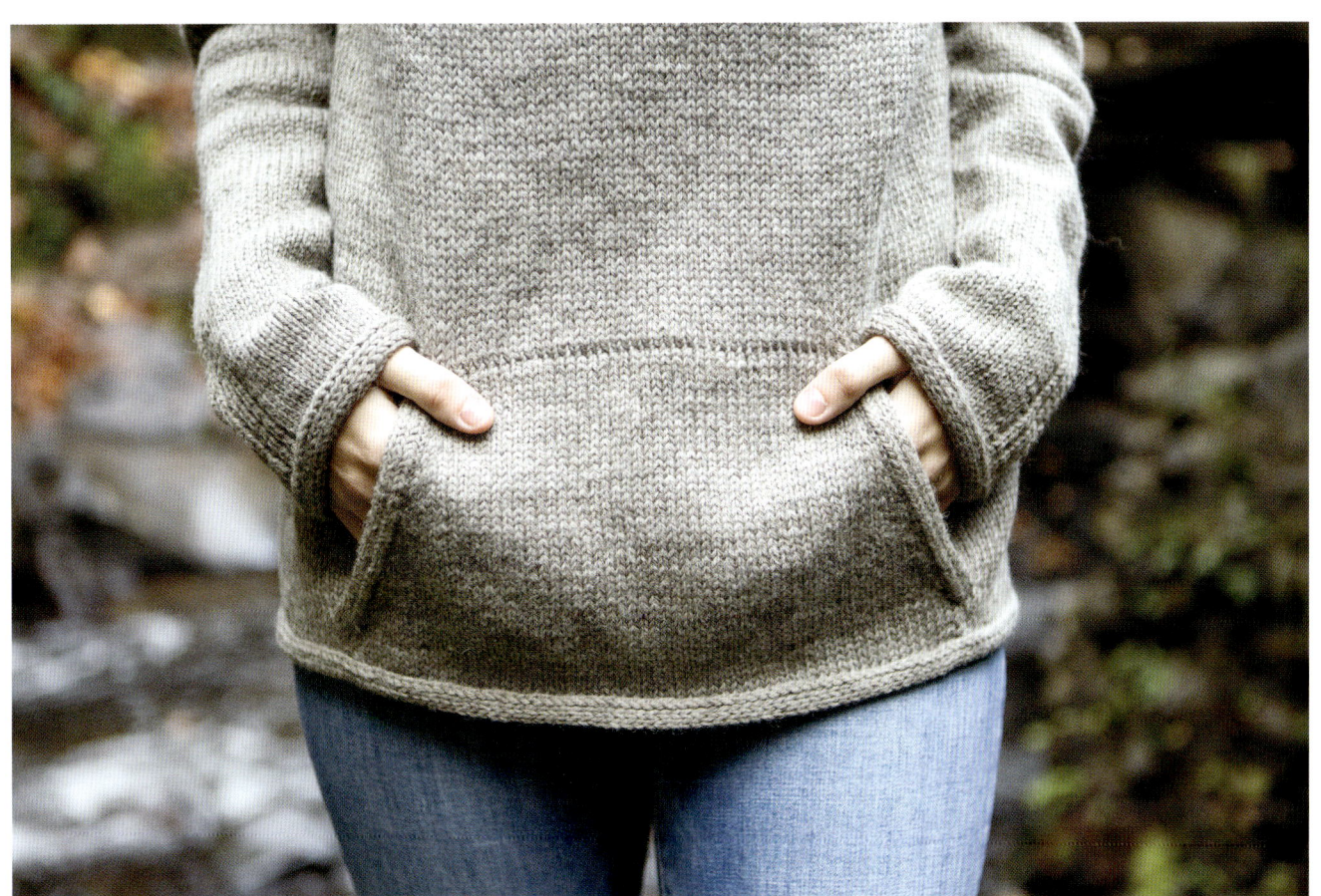

Sleeves (make 2 the same)

Place 71 (71, 73, 83, 87, 95) sts held for sleeve on DPNs, PM for beginning of rnd at center of underarm.

Cont Seeded Rib panel as established, work even in St st for 1".

Sleeve Dec Rnd: K1, K2tog, K to 3 sts before end of rnd, SSK, K1. 2 sts dec.

Rep Sleeve Dec Rnd 9 (8, 9, 11, 12, 16) more times every 9th (9th, 9th, 9th, 8th, 7th) rnd, until 51 (53, 53, 59, 61, 61) sts remain.

Cont Seeded Rib panel as established, WE in St st until sleeve measures 18 (18, 18.5, 20, 21, 22)" from underarm. BO using I-Cord Bind Off.

Funnel Neck

Using shorter circular, with RS facing and beginning at back left shoulder, PU and K 15 (15, 15, 17, 17, 17) sts along left shoulder edge, PU and K 45 (46, 49, 49, 49, 49) sts along front neck edge and PM after 23 (23, 25, 25, 25, 25) sts of front edge, PU and K 15 (15, 15, 17, 17, 17) sts along right shoulder edge and 45 (46, 49, 49, 49, 49) sts along back neck edge. PM and join in the rnd. 120 (122, 128, 132, 132, 132) sts.

WE in St st for 3 (3, 3, 3.5, 3.5, 3.5)".

Casing
Size 46.5" Only

K to first M, turn work and work flat in St st for 3 rows.
Resume working St st in the rnd for 2 rnds.
Purl 1 rnd.
WE in St st for 3 rnds.
BO.

All Other Sizes

K to 2 sts before first M, K2tog, turn work and work flat in St st for 3 rows.
Resume working St st in the rnd for 2 rnds.
Purl 1 rnd.
WE in St st for 2 rnds.
BO.

Finishing

Casing

Turn upper neck edge to inside along purl rnd. Stitch in place.
Work 44" in I-cord for drawstring.
Using large safety pin, thread I-cord drawstring through casing in upper neck edge.

Pocket Edging

Starting at bottom corner, PU and K 42 (42, 42, 49, 49, 49) sts along edge of pocket.
BO using I-Cord BO.
Rep for second pocket edge.

Weave in ends, wash, and block to diagram.

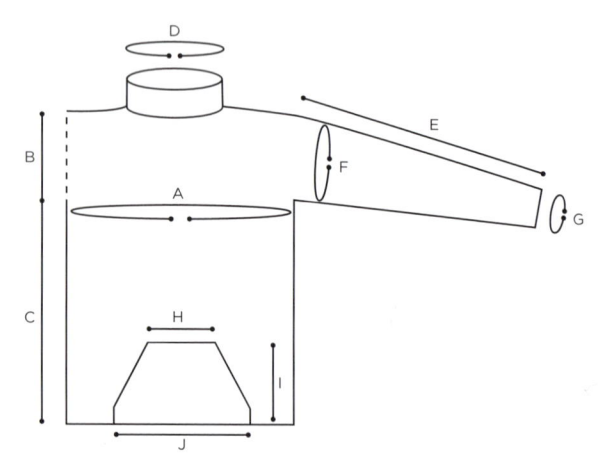

A: 42 (46,5, 50, 54, 58, 62)"
B: 8.5 (9.25, 9.75, 11, 12, 13.25)"
C: 15.5 (15.5, 16, 16.5, 17, 18)"
D: 24 (24.5, 25.5, 26.5, 26.5, 26.5)"
E: 18 (18, 18.5, 20, 21, 22)"
F: 14.25 (14.25, 14.5, 16.5, 17.5, 19)"
G: 10.5 (10.5, 10.5, 11.75, 12, 12)"
H: 7.75 (8, 8.25, 9.75, 9.75, 9.75)"
I: 7.5 (7.5, 7.5, 8, 8, 8)"
J: 11.75 (12, 12.25, 14.25, 14.25, 14.25)"

Slade Pullover

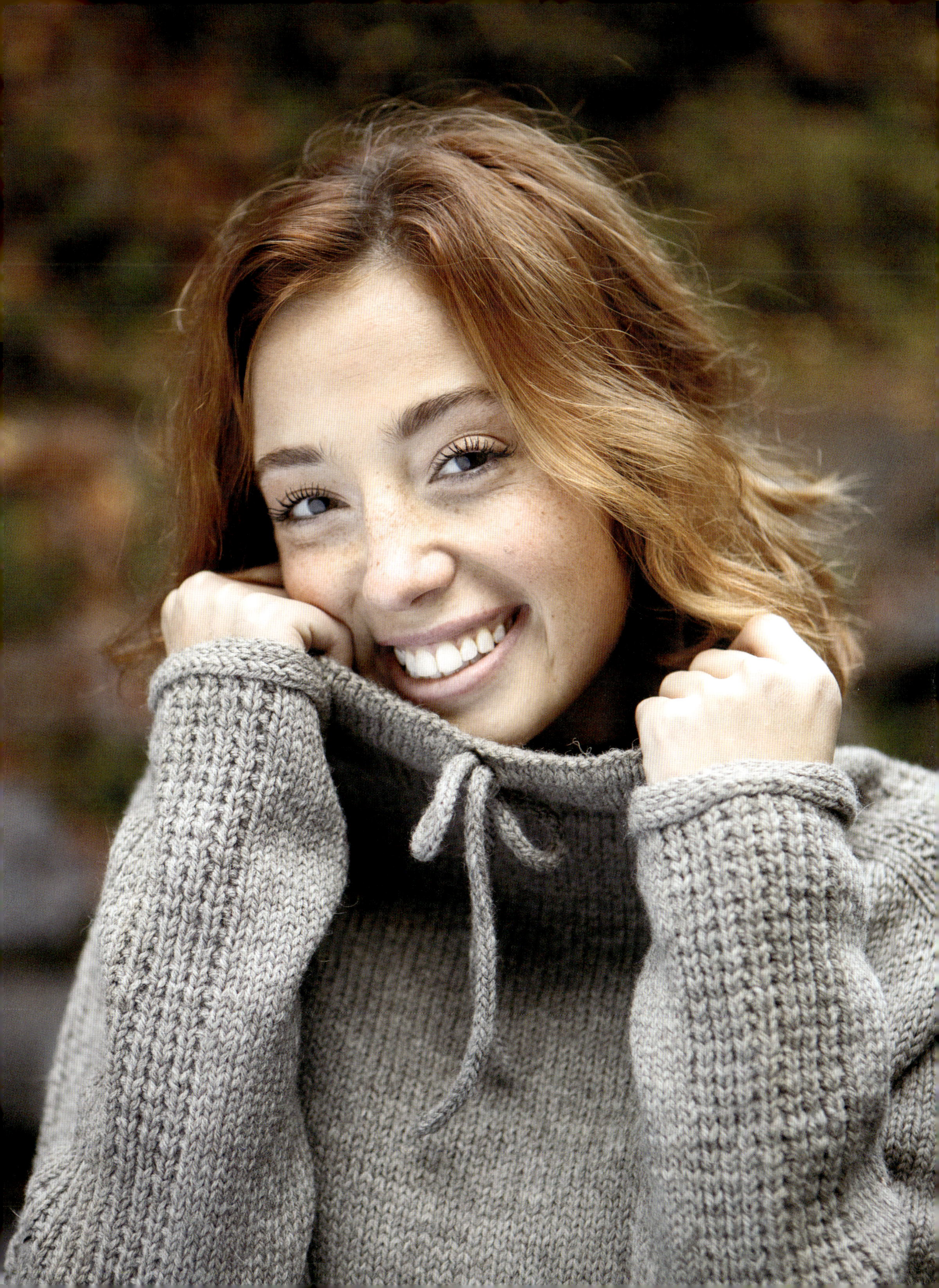

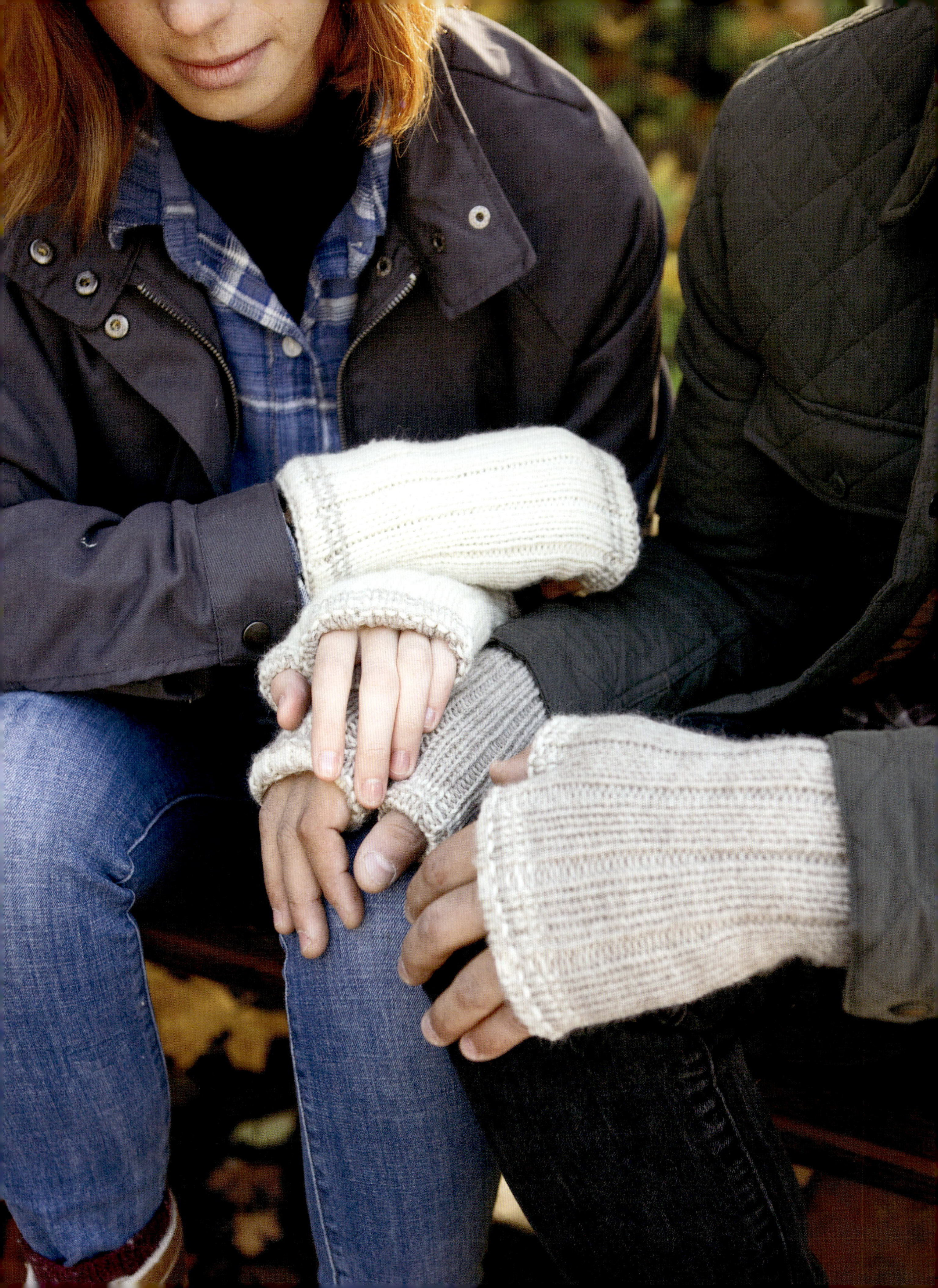

SNUG GLOVES

by Violet LeBeaux

FINISHED MEASUREMENTS
7.5" circumference x 8" length; adjustable

YARN
Knit Picks Simply Wool (worsted weight, 100% Eco Wool; 218 yards/100g): MC Winnie 27470, C1 Wanda 27468, 1 hank each

NEEDLES
US 7 (4.5mm) DPNs or long circular needles for Magic Loop technique, or size to obtain gauge

NOTIONS
Yarn Needle
Stitch Markers
Scrap Yarn or Stitch Holder
Wool Roving to use as interfacing (optional)

GAUGE
20 sts and 28 rows = 4" over 3x1 Rib stitch in the round, blocked

For pattern support, contact violetlebeaux@gmail.com

Snug Gloves

Notes:

Snug is a simple and extremely warm, double layered, unisex fingerless glove pattern. It features a 3x1 Rib, garter stitch edge, and contrast color stripe details. The gloves are double layered for extra warmth. The pattern is versatile and can be customized easily, so everyone in the family can have matching gloves based on their own style.

The construction of the gloves is done in the round with the thumb added afterwards. During the finishing, additional roving or interfacing can be sandwiched inside the gloves to make them unbeatably warm.

3x1 Rib (in the rnd over multiples of 4 sts)
All Rnds: (K3, P1) to end of rnd.

Magic Loop Technique
A technique using one long circular needle to knit in the round with. A tutorial can be found at: http://tutorials.knitpicks.com/wptutorials/magic-loop/.

Sizing Customization Tips
These gloves have a simple construction so they can be customized for multiple hand sizes. To customize the circumference, measure around the widest part of the hand and use your gauge to calculate and round up to the next multiple of 4 sts. If you are adding roving/interfacing, add 0.5" to your hand measurement to account for the added thickness. The ribbing makes the gloves padded and stretchy, so if in doubt of size, go with a larger CO number; e.g., if the hand circumference is 9.5" with a gauge of 5 sts per inch, 9.5 x 5 = 47.5, and round up to the next multiple of 4 = 48. Therefore CO 48 sts.

DIRECTIONS
The gloves are worked in the round from the wrist up.

Gloves (make 2 the same)
Main Section
With MC, loosely CO 40 sts (or a multiple of 4 sts), PM and join to work in the rnd being careful not to twist sts.
Rnds 1-3: With MC, (K3, P1) to end.
Rnd 4: With C1, (K3, P1) to end.
Rnd 5: With MC, (K3, P1) to end.
Rnds 6-7: Rep Rnds 4-5.
Rnds 8-42: With MC rep Rnd 5 35 more times OR until work is 6", or the desired length from edge to beginning of thumb. Place previous 12 sts (or a multiple of 4 sts to customize thumb circumference) on scrap yarn and cont working in the rnd on the remaining 28 sts.
Rnd 43: With MC, (K3, P1) to end.
Rnds 44-50: With MC, rep Rnd 43 seven more times OR until work is 1.25", or 0.75" shorter than the desired length for fingers.
Rnd 51: With C1, (K3, P1) to end.
Rnd 52: With MC, (K3, P1) to end.
Rnd 53: With C1, (K3, P1) to end.
Rnds 54-56: With MC, (K3, P1) to end.
Rnd 57 (Turning Ridge): With C1, P all.
Rnds 58-59: With C1, (K3, P1) to end.
Rnd 60: With MC, (K3, P1) to end.
Rnd 61: With C1, (K3, P1) to end.
Rnds 62-63: Rep Rnds 60-61.
Rnds 64-69: Rep Rnd 61 six more times OR until work is 2"

from Turning Ridge, or until the same as the desired length for fingers.

Rnd 70: With C1, (K3, P1) to end, CO 12 sts to right needle (or the same number of sts placed on hold after Rnd 42 if customizing). 40 sts.

Rnd 71: With C1, (K3, P1) to end.

Rnds 72-106: Rep Rnd 71 35 more times OR 0.75" shorter than length from CO edge to Turning Ridge, or until work is the same as the desired length from edge to beginning of thumb.

Rnd 107: With MC, (K3, P1) to end.

Rnd 108: With C1, (K3, P1) to end.

Rnd 109: With MC, (K3, P1) to end.

Rnds 110-112: With C1, (K3, P1) to end.

BO all sts.

Thumb Section

Place the 12 sts on hold back onto the needles and PU and K 4 sts from the gap where the thumb meets the rest of the glove, PM and join to work in the rnd. 16 sts.

Rnd 1: With MC, (K3, P1) to end.

Rnds 2-3: Rep Rnd 1 two more times OR until work is the desired length from beginning of thumb to knuckle.

Rnd 4: With C1, (K3, P1) to end.

Rnd 5: With MC, (K3, P1) to end.

Rnds 6-7: Rep Rnds 4-5.

Rnd 8 (Turning Ridge): With C1, P all.

Rnd 9: With MC, (K3, P1) to end.

Rnds 10-11: Rep Rnds 4-5.

Rnds 12-14: Rep Rnd 4 three more times OR until work is the same as the length from PU sts to Turning Ridge, or as the desired length from beginning of thumb to knuckle.

BO all sts.

Finishing

Fold the glove in half so the C1 section is on the inside and the thumb is on the outside. If desired add roving or interfacing between the layers for extra warmth.
Sew the CO and BO edge together. Fold the C1 section of the Thumb inside itself. Turn the whole glove inside out and sew the BO edge to the CO edge of the Thumb.

Weave in ends, wash, and block to finished measurements.

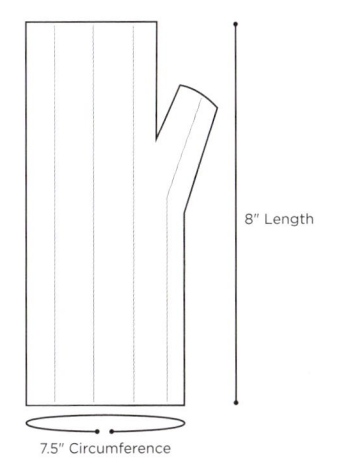

8" Length

7.5" Circumference

Snug Gloves 67

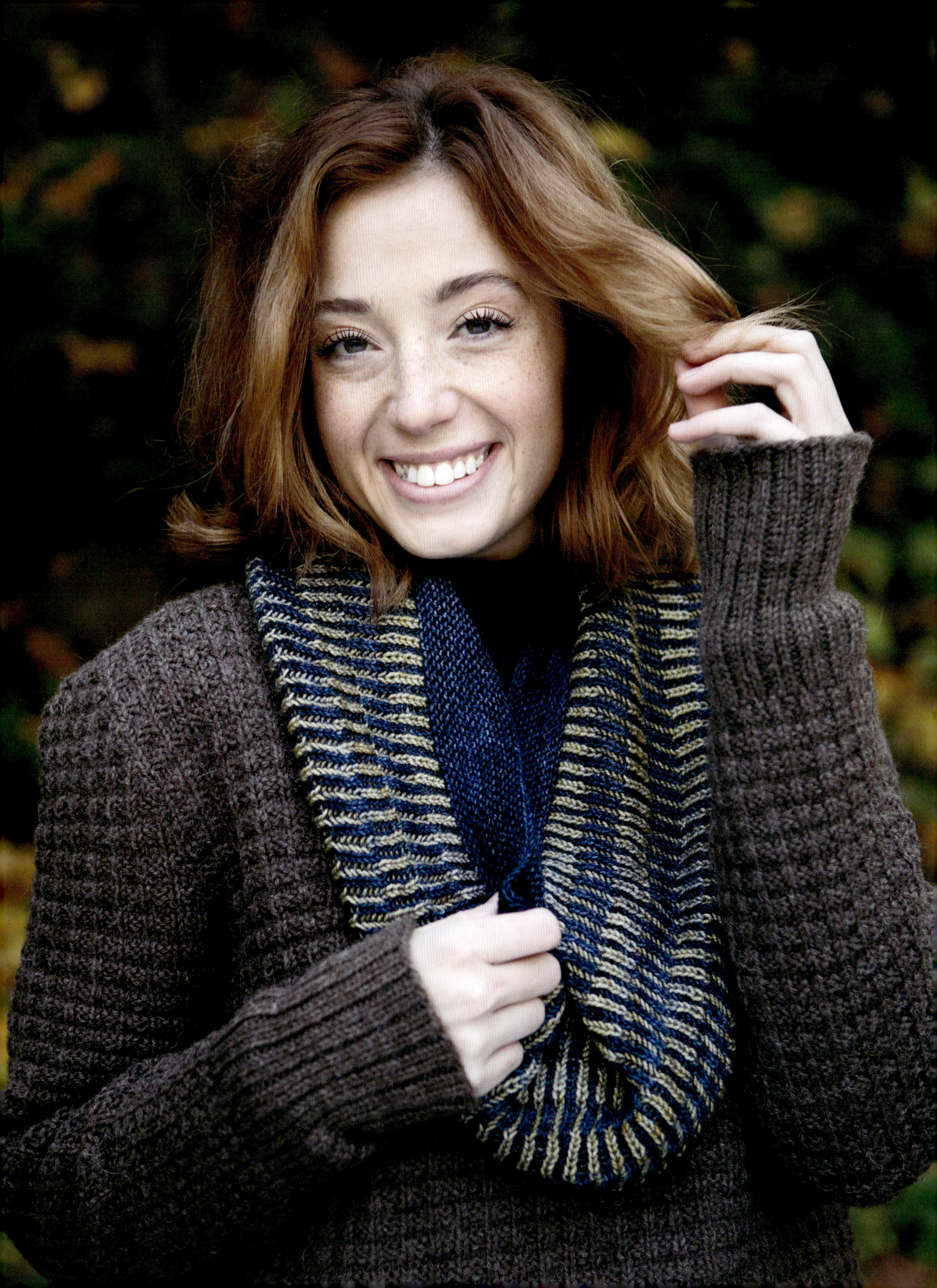

SYNCOPATED BRIOCHE COWL

by Nona Davenport

FINISHED MEASUREMENTS
24 (32)" circumference, 10" wide, unblocked

YARN
Knit Picks Hawthorne Tonal Hand Paint (fingering weight, 80% Superwash Fine Highland Wool, 20% Polyamide (Nylon) (357 yards/100g): DC Klamath Falls 27404, 1 hank
Knit Picks Hawthorne Multi (fingering weight, 80% Superwash Fine Highland Wool, 20% Polyamide (Nylon) (357 yards/100g): LC Portsmouth 27420, 1 hank

NEEDLES
US 3 (3.25mm) 16" circular needles, or size to obtain gauge
US 4 (3.5mm) 16" circular needles, or size to obtain gauge

NOTIONS
Yarn Needle
Stitch Markers

GAUGE
24 sts and 48 rows = 4" in garter stitch in the round on larger needles, unblocked
24 sts and 24 rows (48 passes) = 4" in Simple Brioche Stitch in the round on smaller needles, unblocked

For pattern support, contact nonapearl@firebin.net

Syncopated Brioche Cowl

Notes:
This pattern is worked in the round. The garter sections are worked normally: one pass over the stitches equals one round. In the brioche sections, two passes equals one round.

The brioche sections in this pattern also use "syncopation", a brioche technique where the raised colored sections switch position when stitches that were brioche knit are brioche purled, and vice versa.

Much thanks to Nancy Marchant for her work with the brioche stitch. You can read more at www.briochestitch.com.

Brioche has abbreviations and stitches unique to the technique:

LC = Light Color: Use the light-colored yarn.
DC = Dark Color: Use the dark colored yarn.
LS = Light Side: The side of the knitted fabric where the raised k sts are in the LC yarn.
DS = Dark Side: The side of the knitted fabric where the raised k sts are in the DC yarn.

BRK (Brioche K st)
K the st that was SL in the previous row tog with its YO.

BRP (Brioche P st)
P the st that was SL in the previous row tog with its YO.

SL1YO (SL one with a YO)
This st is performed by bringing the yarn to the front of your work, SL the next st as if to P, and then bringing the yarn to the back of the work by yarning over the SL st. 2 loops are created on the needle when performing a SL1YO, but it still counts only as one st. The yarn must be in the front of the work BEFORE slipping for this st to be worked correctly.

Working the Brioche Stitch: Brioche rows are worked in pairs. It takes 2 complete passes over all of the sts to equal 1 row. When working two-colored brioche (as in this pattern), work one pass in the LC yarn and one pass in the DC yarn for every row counted.

The "flow" for working brioche is different when working a BRK pass vs. a BRP pass.
BRK Flow: *Bring yarn to the front of work between the needles, SL1YO, BRK**; rep from * to **.
BRP Flow: *BRP, (the working yarn is already in the front), SL1YO, bring the yarn back to the front**; rep from * to **.

When working brioche in the rnd, DO NOT twist the working yarns at the end of the row. If you have been working a BRK pass, simply drop the yarn to the back of the work.
PU the new color from the front and begin working the next BRP pass as instructed.
If you have been working a BRP pass, simply drop the yarn to the front of the work.
PU the new color from the back and begin working the next BRK pass as instructed.

Garter Stitch (in the rnd over any number of sts)
Rnd 1 and all odd Rnds: K all.
Rnd 2 and all even Rnds: P all.
Rep Rnds 1-2 for pattern.

Syncopated Brioche Stitch Pattern (in the rnd)
Section 1 (Rnds 1-6)
Rnd 1 LC: *BRK, SL1YO; rep from * to end of rnd. Let working yarn hang to the back at the end of the pass.
Rnd 1 DC: *SL1YO, BRP; rep from * to end of rnd. Let working yarn hang to the front at the end of the pass.
Rnds 2-6: Rep both passes of Rnd 1 five more times.
Section 2 (Rnds 7-12)
Rnd 7 LC: *BRP, SL1YO; rep from * to end of rnd. Let working yarn hang to the front at the end of the pass.
Rnd 7 DC: *SL1YO, BRK; rep from * to end of rnd. Let working yarn hang to the back at the end of the pass.
Rnds 8-12: Rep both passes of Rnd 7 five more times.

DIRECTIONS

Loosely CO 144 (192) sts in DC on larger needles. Join to work in the rnd, being careful not to twist sts. PM for beg of rnd.

Rnds 1-20: Work garter stitch.

Switch to smaller needles.

Brioche Set Up Rnd DC: *SL1YO, P1; rep from * to end of rnd. Let working yarn hang to the front at the end of the pass.

Rnds 21-56: Work Syncopated Brioche Stitch Pattern 3 times.
Rnds 57-61: Work Rnds 1-5 of Syncopated Brioche Stitch Pattern.
Rnd 62 LC: *BRK, SL1YO; rep from * to end of rnd. Let working yarn hang to the back at the end of the pass. Break yarn.
Rnd 62 DC: *BRK, K1; rep from * to end of rnd.

Switch to larger needles.

Rnd 63-83: Work garter stitch.

Finishing

Weave in ends, wash, and block gently if desired. Blocking brioche too aggressively detracts from the wonderful squishy texture.

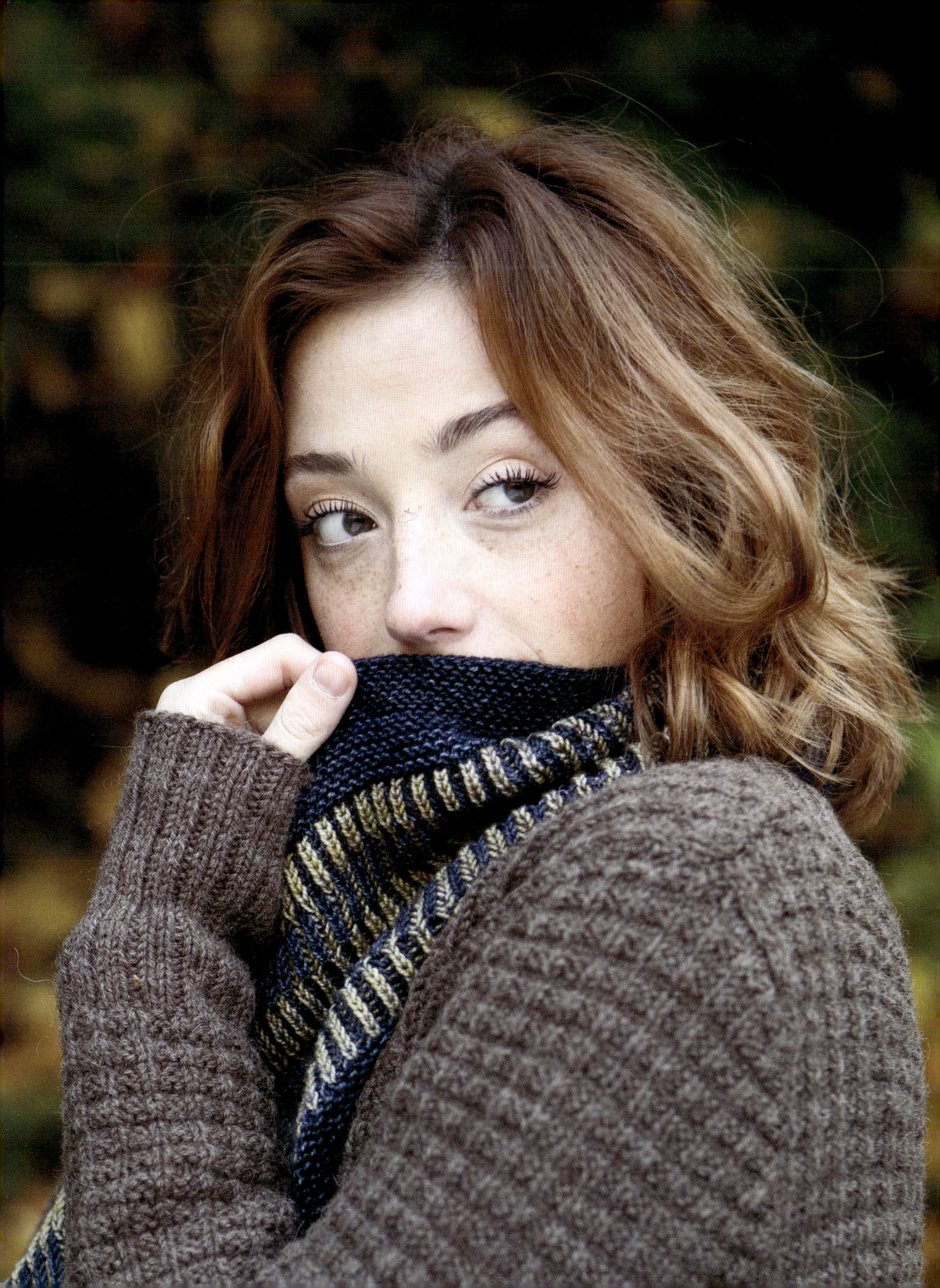

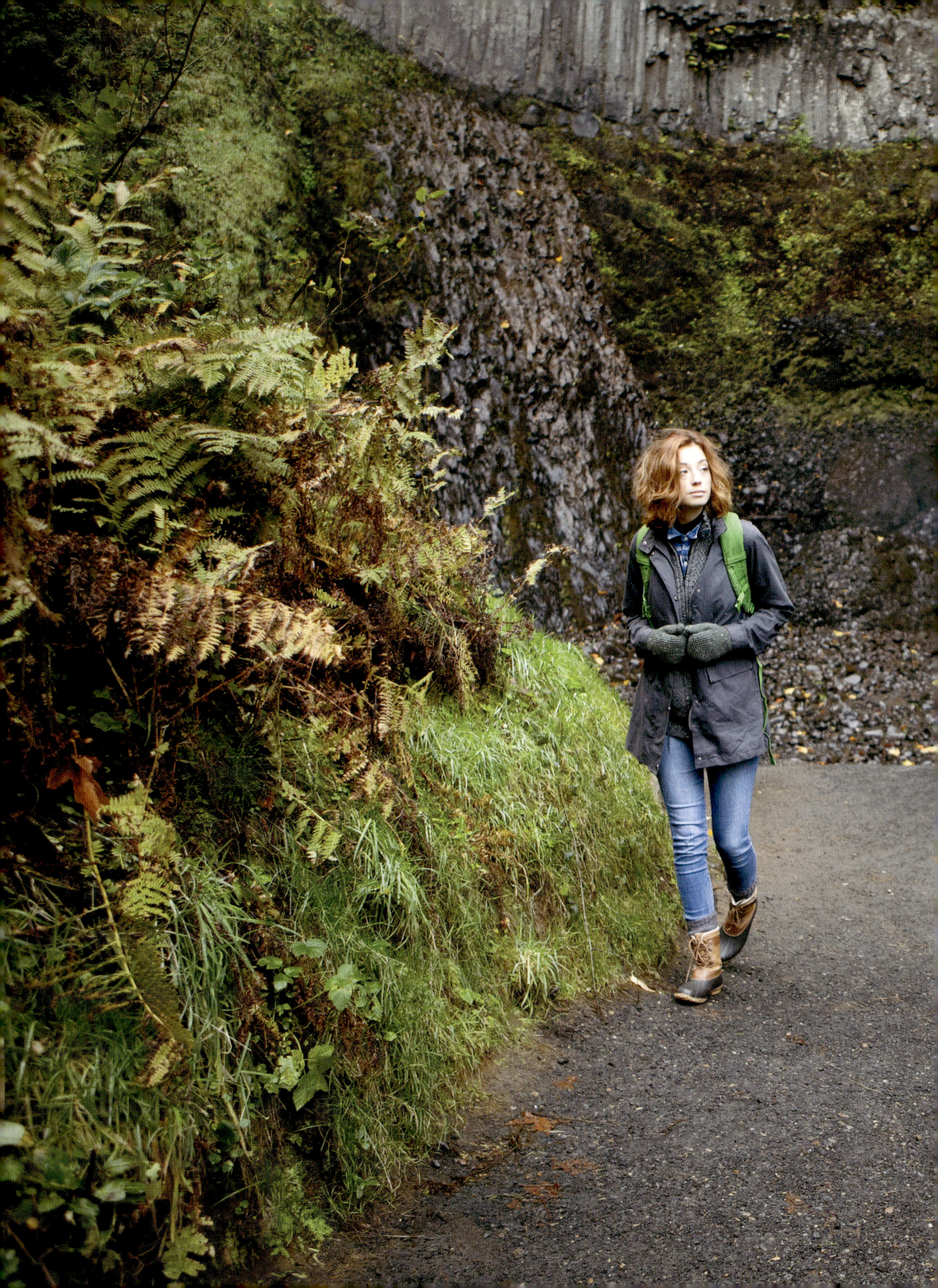

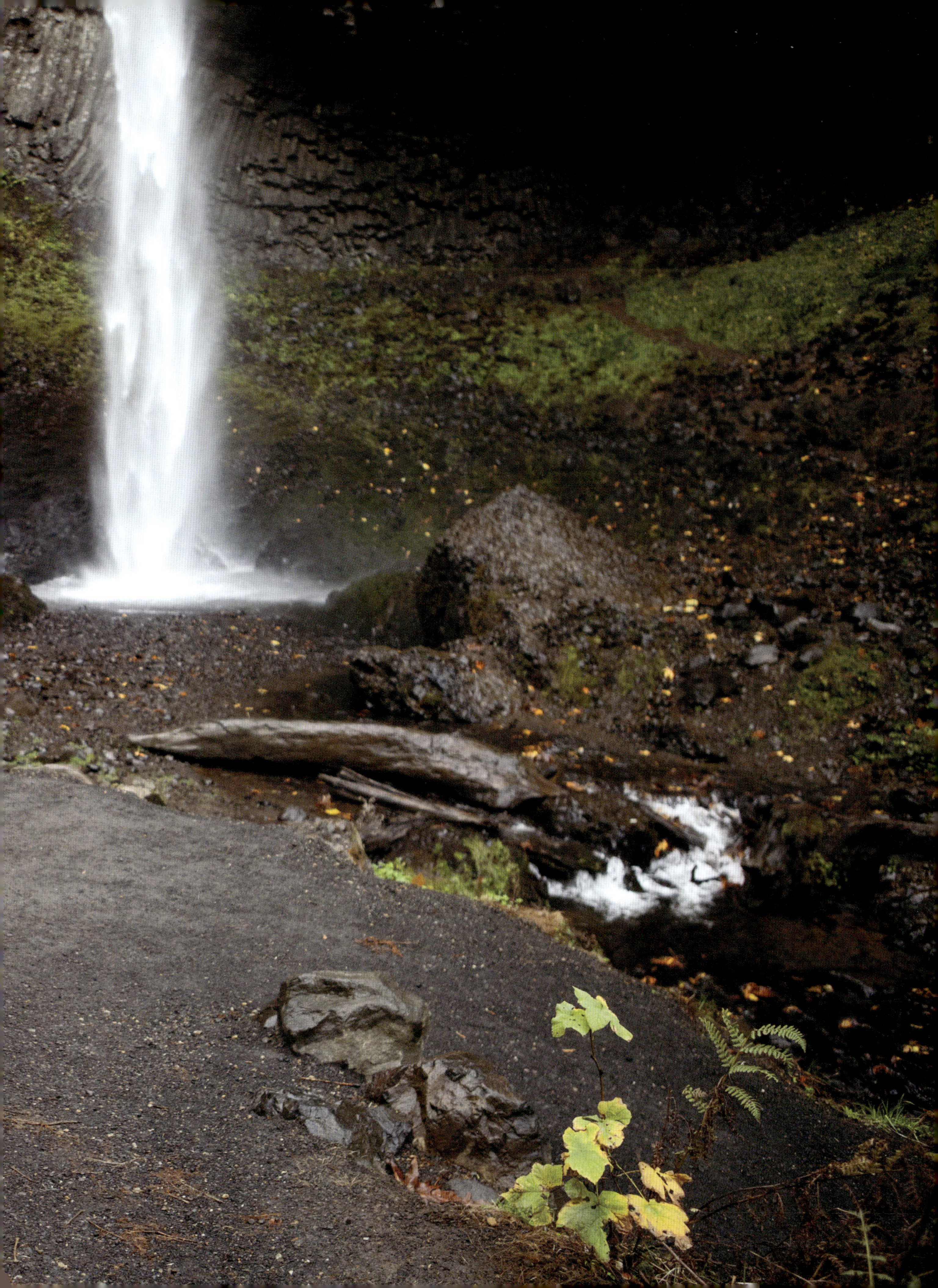

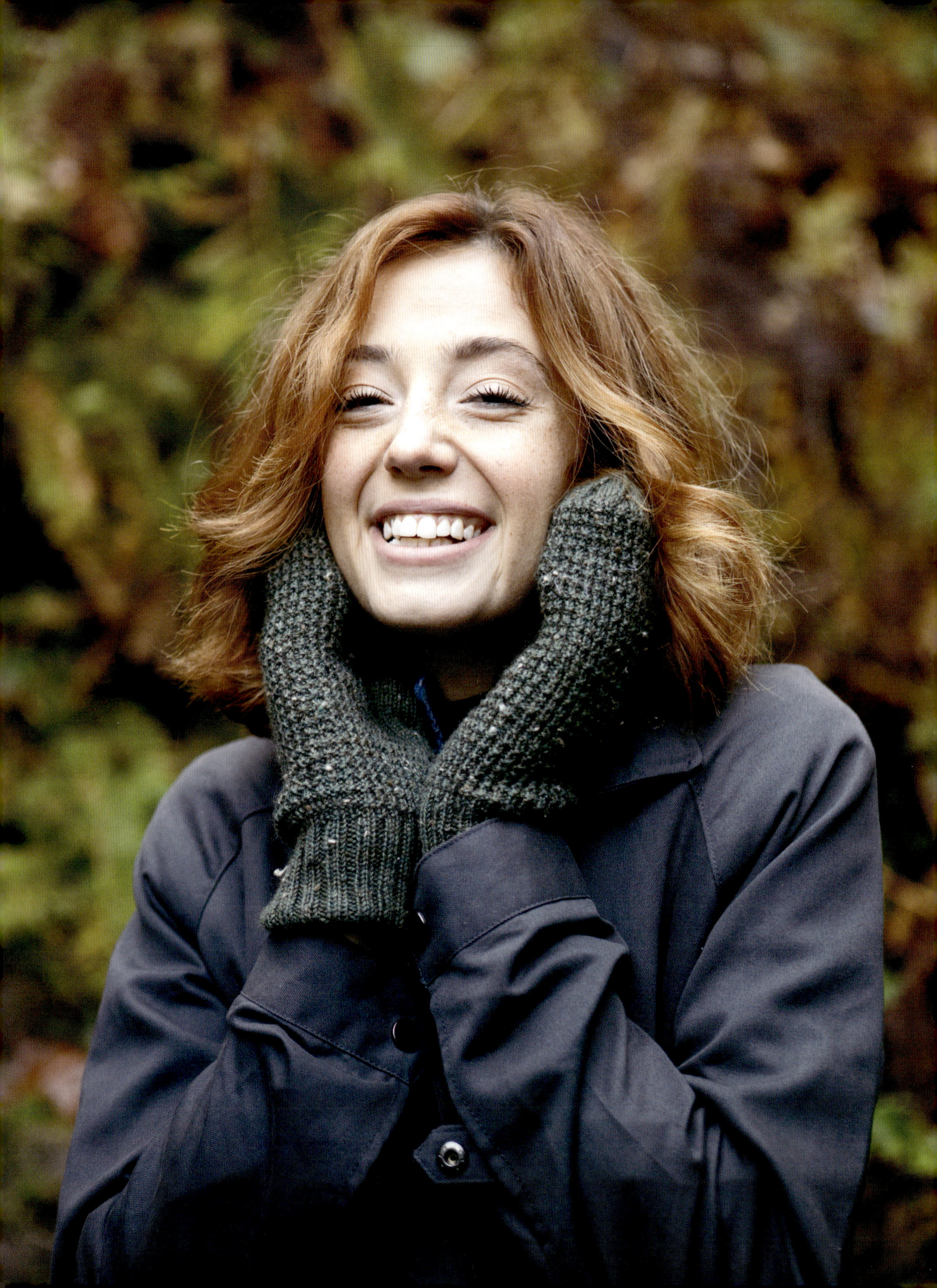

TIMBERLINE MITTENS

by Emily Kintigh

FINISHED MEASUREMENTS
7 (7.5, 8, 8.5)" finished hand circumference

YARN
Knit Picks Stroll Tweed (fingering weight, 65% Fine Superwash Merino Wool, 25% Nylon, 10% Donegal; 231 yards/50g): C1 Lost Lake Heather 26295, 2 balls; C2 Oyster Heather 26281, 1 skein

NEEDLES
US 1 (2.25mm) DPNs or two 24" circular needles for two circulars technique, or one 32" or longer circular needle for Magic Loop technique, or one size less than size to obtain gauge

US 2 (2.75mm) DPNs or two 24" circular needles for two circulars technique, or one 32" or longer circular needle for Magic Loop technique, or size to obtain gauge

NOTIONS
Yarn Needle
Stitch Markers
Scrap Yarn or Stitch Holder

GAUGE
32 sts and 42 rows = 4" in stockinette stitch in the round on larger needles, blocked

For pattern support, contact auntieemsstudio@gmail.com

Timberline Mittens

Notes:
The mittens and lining are worked separately and then sewn together. The mitten will be slightly bigger than the finished hand measurements so that the lining can fit comfortably inside. The lining measurements will match the size measurements.

The waffle pattern on the mitten will pull the fabric in and make it narrower until it is blocked.

Waffle Pattern (in the rnd over an even number of sts)
Rnds 1-2: (K1, P1) to end.
Rnd 3: P all.
Rep Rnds 1-3 for pattern.

Stockinette Stitch (St st, in the rnd over any number of sts)
All Rnds: K to end.

2x2 Rib (in the rnd over multiples of 4 sts)
All Rnds: (K2, P2) to end.

DIRECTIONS

Mittens: Cuff
With smaller needles and C1, loosely CO 60 (64, 68, 72) sts. PM and join in the rnd being careful not to twist the sts. Work in 2x2 Ribbing for 4.5 (5, 5.5, 6)".
Switch to larger needles.
Next Rnd: (K1, P1) to end.

Mittens: Thumb Gusset
Rnd 1: M1R, PM, (K1, P1) to end. 61 (65, 69, 73) sts.
Rnd 2: K to M, SM, P to end.
Rnd 3: M1L, K to M, M1R, SM, (K1, P1) to end. 63 (67, 71, 75) sts.
Rnd 4: K to M, SM, (K1, P1) to end.
Rnd 5: M1L, K to M, M1R, SM, P to end. 65 (69, 73, 77) sts.
Rnd 6: K to M, SM, (K1, P1) to end.
Rnd 7: Rep Rnd 3. 67 (71, 75, 79) sts.
Rep Rnds 2-7 three more times. 85 (89, 93, 97) sts.

7" Size
Work Rnd 2 once more.
Next Rnd: Place next 25 sts on scrap yarn to be worked later for the thumb, remove M, (K1, P1) to end. 60 sts.

7.5" and 8" Sizes
Work Rnds 2-4 once more.
Next Rnd: Place next 27 sts on scrap yarn to be worked later for the thumb, remove M, P to end. 64 (68) sts.

8.5" Size
Work Rnds 2-6 once more.
Next Rnd: Place next 29 sts on scrap yarn to be worked later for the thumb, remove M, (K1, P1) to end. 72 sts.

Mittens: Main Mitten
Work in Waffle Pattern beginning with Rnd 2 (1, 1, 3) of stitch pattern until mitten measures 6.25 (6.75, 7.5, 8)" from top of cuff and ending with Rnd 2 of stitch pattern.
Knit 1 rnd then move on to Decreases.

Decreases
7" Size: (K13, K2tog) to end. 56 sts. Cont with Decreases beginning with Rnd 4.
7.5" Size: Begin working Rnd 3 of Decreases.
8" Size: (K15, K2tog) to end. 64 sts. Cont with Decreases beginning with Rnd 2.
8.5" Size: Begin working Rnd 1 of Decreases.

Rnd 1: (K7, K2tog) to end. 64 sts.
Rnd 2: K all.
Rnd 3: (K6, K2tog) to end. 56 sts.
Rnd 4: K all.
Rnd 5: (K5, K2tog) to end. 48 sts.
Rnd 6: K all.
Rnd 7: (K4, K2tog) to end. 40 sts.
Rnd 8: K all.
Rnd 9: (K3, K2tog) to end. 32 sts.
Rnd 10: K all.
Rnd 11: (K2, K2tog) to end. 24 sts.
Rnd 12: K all.
Rnd 13: (K1, K2tog) to end. 16 sts.
Rnd 14: K all.
Rnd 15: K2tog to end. 8 sts.
Cut yarn and pull through remaining sts.

Mittens: Thumb
Place 25 (27, 27, 29) held sts on larger needles. PM and rejoin C1 to begin working in the rnd.
Rnd 1: K2tog, K to end. 24 (26, 26, 28) sts.
Work in St st until thumb measures 2.25 (2.5, 2.75, 3)".

Thumb Decreases
7" Size
Rnd 1: (K2, K2tog) to end. 18 sts.
Rnd 2: K all.

7.5" and 8" Sizes
Rnd 1: *(K1, K2tog) three times, K2, K2tog; rep from * to end. 18 sts.
Rnd 2: K all.

8.5" Size
Rnd 1: (K5, K2tog) to end. 24 sts.
Rnd 2: (K2, K2tog) to end. 18 sts.

All Sizes
Rnd 3: (K1, K2tog) to end. 12 sts.
Rnd 4: K2tog to end. 6 sts.
Cut yarn and pull through remaining sts.

Lining
With larger needles and C2, loosely CO 56 (60, 64, 68) sts. PM and join to work in the rnd being careful not to twist the sts.
Knit 1 rnd.

Lining: Thumb Gusset

Rnd 1: M1R, PM, K to end. 57 (61, 65, 69) sts.
Rnd 2: K all.
Rnd 3: M1L, K to M, M1R, SM, K to end. 59 (63, 67, 71) sts.
Rep Rnds 2-3 10 (11, 11, 12) more times, then Rnd 2 once more. 79 (85, 89, 95) sts.

Next Rnd: Place next 23 (25, 25, 27) sts on holder to be worked later for the thumb, remove M, K to end. 56 (60, 64, 68) sts.

Lining: Main Mitten

Work in St st until piece measures 6 (6.5, 7.25, 7.75)" from CO edge.

Decreases

7" Size: Begin working Rnd 3 of Decreases.
7.5" Size: (K13, K2tog) to end. 56 sts. Cont with Decreases beginning with Rnd 2.
8" Size: Begin working Rnd 1 of Decreases.
8.5" Size: (K15, K2tog) to end. 64 sts. Cont with Decreases beginning with Rnd 1.

Rnd 1: (K6, K2tog) to end. 56 sts.
Rnds 2, 4, 6, 8, 10, 12: K all.
Rnd 3: (K5, K2tog) to end. 48 sts.
Rnd 5: (K4, K2tog) to end. 40 sts.
Rnd 7: (K3, K2tog) to end. 32 sts.
Rnd 9: (K2, K2tog) to end. 24 sts.
Rnd 11: (K1, K2tog) to end. 16 sts.
Rnd 13: K2tog to end. 8 sts.
Cut yarn and pull through remaining sts.

Lining: Thumb

Place 23 (25, 25, 27) held sts on larger needles. PM and rejoin C2 to begin working in the rnd.
Rnd 1: K2tog, K to end. 22 (24, 24, 26) sts.
Work in St st until thumb measures 2 (2.25, 2.5, 2.75)".

Thumb Decreases

7" Size
Rnd 1: (K3, K2tog, K4, K2tog) to end. 18 sts.

7.5" and 8" Sizes
Rnd 1: (K2, K2tog) to end. 18 sts.
Rnd 2: K all.

8.5" Size
Rnd 1: *(K1, K2tog) three times, K2, K2tog; rep from * to end. 18 sts.
Rnd 2: K all.

All Sizes
Next Rnd: (K1, K2tog) to end. 12 sts.
Next Rnd: K2tog to end. 6 sts.
Cut yarn and pull through remaining sts.

Finishing

Weave in ends making sure to close up gaps between the thumb and hand. Block outer mitten to 7.5 (8, 8.5, 9)" circumference and lining to 7 (7.5, 8, 8.5)" circumference. Turn the lining inside out and place inside mitten so that the wrong sides are together. Fold the cuff so that the CO edge of the main mitten meets the CO edge of the lining. Using C1, sew the two CO edges together. Weave in ends.

Timberline Mittens

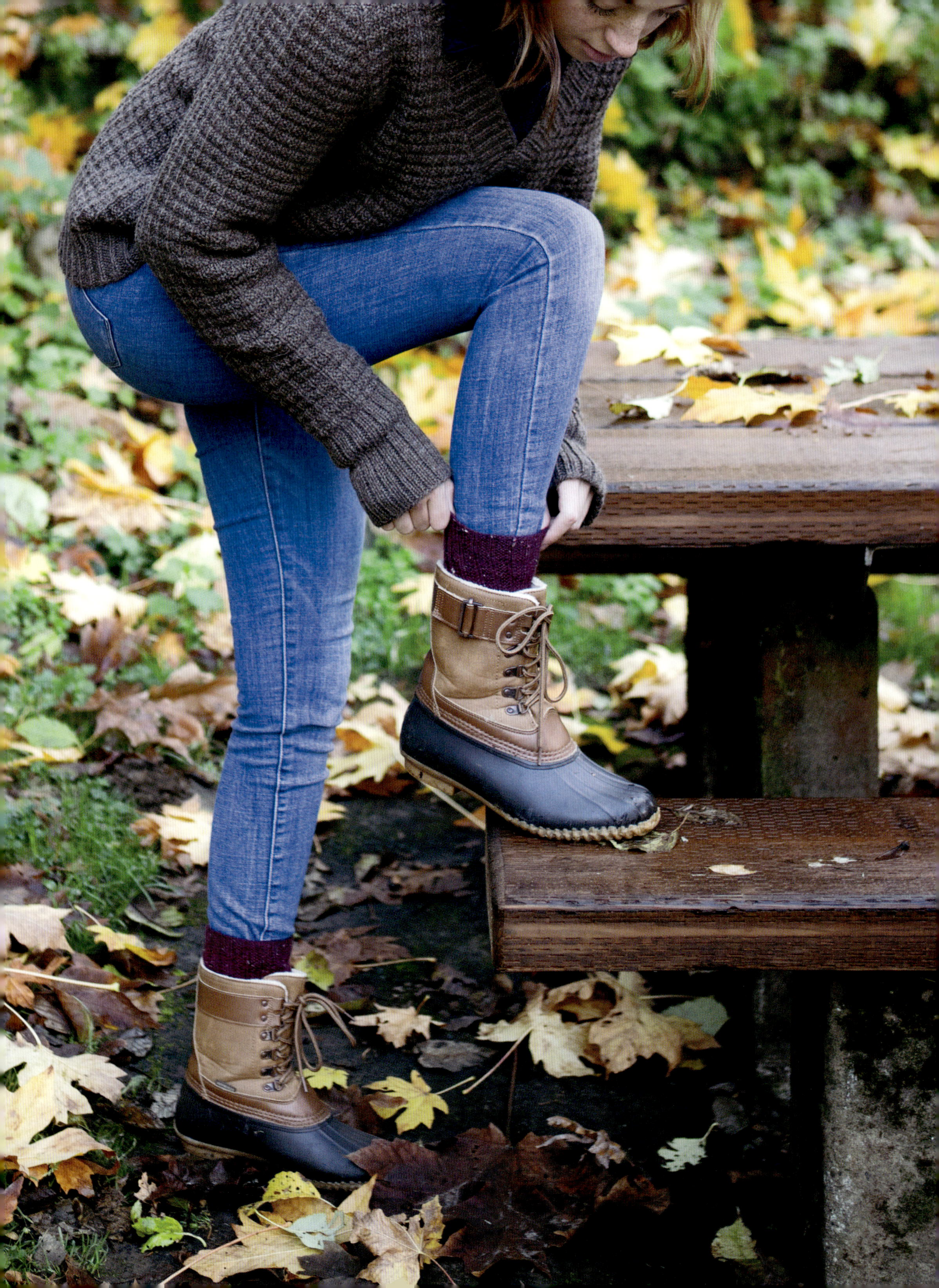

TRAILHEAD SOCKS

by Mone Dräger

FINISHED MEASUREMENTS
7 (8, 9)" leg and foot circumference, 9.25 (9.75, 10)" leg length with cuff unfolded, including heel; foot and leg length are adjustable

YARN
Knit Picks Stroll Tweed (fingering weight, 65% Superwash Merino Wool, 25% Nylon, 10% Donegal Tweed; 231 yards/50g): Barn Door Heather 26297, 2 skeins

NEEDLES
US 1.5 (2.5mm) DPNs or two 24" circular needles for two circulars technique, or one 32" or longer circular needle for Magic Loop technique, or size to obtain gauge

US 1 (2.25mm) DPNs or two 24" circular needles for two circulars technique, or one 32" or longer circular needle for Magic Loop technique, or one size smaller than size to obtain gauge

NOTIONS
Yarn Needle
Stitch Markers

GAUGE
32 sts and 44 rows = 4" in Double Garter Rib in the round on larger needles, lightly blocked
32 sts and 44 rows = 4" in stockinette stitch in the round on larger needles, lightly blocked

For pattern support, contact mone.draeger@gmx.de

Trailhead Socks

Notes:
The great fit of these socks, in an all-over double garter rib pattern, will make these your go-to socks for any outdoor adventure. The cuff is worked extra long to be folded down over your boots, but could be worn unfolded when an extra-long sock and extra warmth is needed. The hybrid Fleegle heel emerges neatly from the ribbing. It is integrated in the leg and worked in rounds, making it seamless and comfortable to wear in any shoes.

Double Garter Rib (worked in the rnd over a multiple of 4 sts)
Rnd 1: K all.
Rnd 2: (K2, P2) to end.
Note: Worked on the instep, the pattern starts and ends within the rep. Keep all instep sts as established in pattern.

Right Lifted Increase (RLI)
Insert the tip of the RH needle from back to front into the st in the row below the next st on the LH needle and lift this st onto the LH needle, then K into it.

Left Lifted Increase (LLI)
Insert the tip of the LH needle from back to front into the st two rows below the st on the RH needle and K TBL.

Knit Into Stitch Below Increase
See a tutorial on lifted increases (K into st below increases) here: https://tutorials.knitpicks.com/knit-into-stitch-below/.

Kitchener Stitch
With an equal number of sts on two needles, thread end of working yarn through yarn needle. Hold needles parallel with RS facing and both needles pointing to the right. Perform Step 2 on the first front st, and then Step 4 on the first back st, and then continue with instructions below.
Step 1: Pull yarn needle K-wise though front st and drop st from knitting needle.
Step 2: Pull yarn needle P-wise through next front st, leave st on knitting needle.
Step 3: Pull yarn needle P-wise through first back st and drop st from knitting needle.
Step 4: Pull yarn needle K-wise through next back st, leave st on knitting needle.
Rep Steps 1–4 until all sts have been grafted.

A tutorial for the Kitchener Stitch can be found at: https://tutorials.knitpicks.com/kitchener-stitch/.

DIRECTIONS
Cuff and Leg
With larger needles, loosely CO 56 (64, 72) sts. Join to work in the rnd, PM, being careful not to twist sts.
Work in Double Garter Rib for 24 rnds.
Change to smaller needles and work in Double Garter Rib for 50 rnds or to desired length to the heel.

Heel
Integrated Heel
Cont to work in the rnd.
Rnd 1: RLI, K2, LLI, PM, K to end. 2 sts inc.
Rnd 2: K to M, P2, (K2, P2)to end.
Rnd 3: RLI, K to M, LLI, SM, K to end. 2 sts inc.
Rep Rnds 2-3 12 (14, 16) more times; then rep Rnd 2 once more. 84 (96, 108) sts..

Turn the Heel
The turn of the heel will be worked flat in rows over the first 43 (49, 55) sts and the last 13 (15, 17) sts of the rnd; total of 56 (64, 72) sts for the heel. Keep remaining 28 (32, 36) sts on hold for instep and rearrange sts on needles accordingly if desired.
Short-Row 1 (RS): K18 (20, 22), SSK, K1, turn. 1 st dec.
Short-Row 2 (WS): SL1 WYIF, P7, P2tog, P1, turn. 1 st dec.
Short-Row 3: SL1 WYIB, K to 1 st before the gap, SSK, K1, turn. 1 st dec.
Short-Row 4: SL1 WYIF, P to 1 st before the gap, P2tog, P1, turn. 1 st dec.
Rep Short-Rows 3-4 8 (10, 12) more times. 28 (32, 36) sts between the gaps, 4 sts on either side of the gaps.
Next Short-Row: SL1 WYIB, K to 1 st before the gap, SSK, turn. 1 st dec.
Next Short-Row: SL1 WYIF, P to 1 st before the gap, P2tog, turn. 1 st dec.
Rep last 2 rows two more times. 28 (32, 36) sts between the gaps, 1 st on either side of the gaps.

Foot
Resume working in the rnd.
Setup Rnd: SL1 WYIB, K to 1 st before the gap, SSK, PM for beginning of rnd, work in Double Garter Rib as established across 28 (32, 36) instep sts, PM, K2tog, K to end. 56 (64, 72) sts total; 28 (32, 36) each on instep and sole.
Next Rnd: Work to M in Double Garter Rib, SM, K to end.
Rep last rnd until foot measures 1.75 (2, 2.5)" less than the desired foot length.

Toe
Rnds 1-3: K all.
Rnd 4: *K1, SSK, K to 3 sts before M, K2tog, K1; rep from * once more. 4 sts dec.
Rnds 5-6: K all.
Rnd 7: *K1, SSK, K to 3 sts before M, K2tog, K1; rep from * once. 4 sts dec.
Rnd 8: K all.
Rep Rnds 7-8 3 (5, 7) more times. 36 sts.
Rep Rnd 7 five more times. 16 sts.
Cut yarn, leaving an 18" tail.

Finishing
Use the yarn needle and tail and graft the instep sts to the toe sts, using the Kitchener Stitch.
Weave in ends, wash, and block lightly.

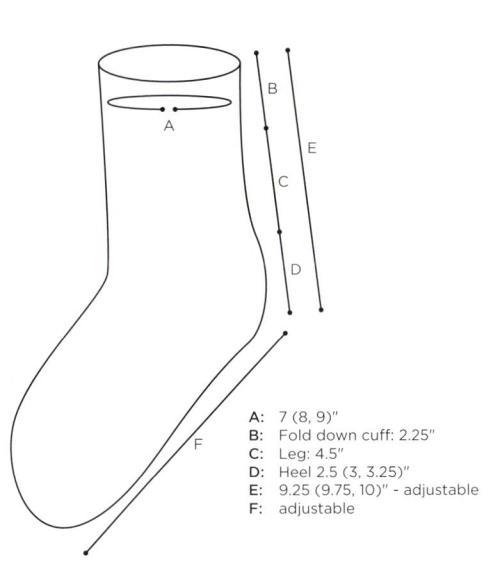

A: 7 (8, 9)"
B: Fold down cuff: 2.25"
C: Leg: 4.5"
D: Heel 2.5 (3, 3.25)"
E: 9.25 (9.75, 10)" - adjustable
F: adjustable

Trailhead Socks 81

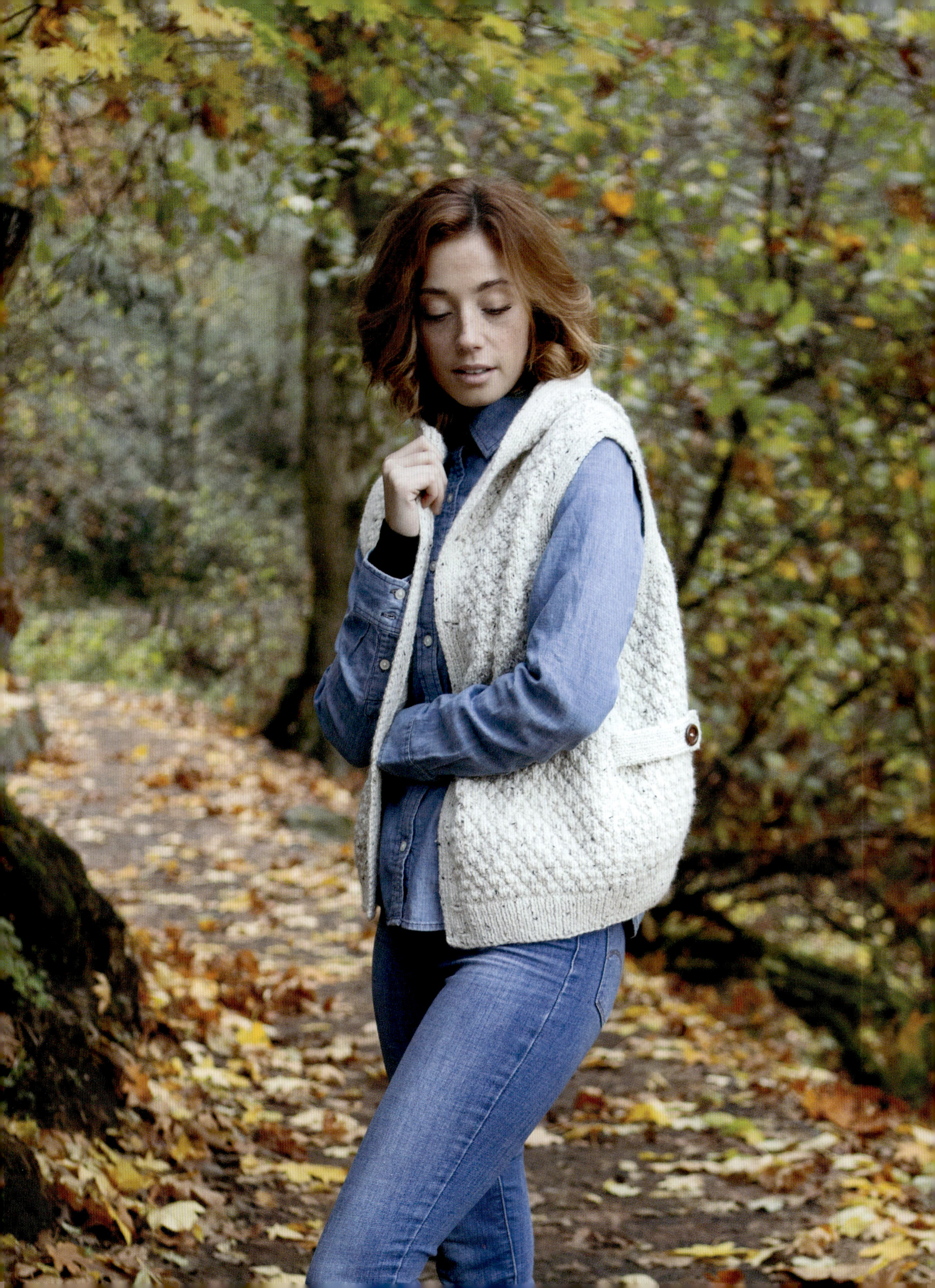

VALEN

by Maria Leigh

FINISHED MEASUREMENT
37 (40, 43, 46, 49)" finished bust measurement; garment is meant to be worn with 6" of ease

YARN
Knit Picks Woodland Tweed (Aran weight, 80% Merino Wool, 15% Baby Alpaca, 5% Viscose; 180 yards/100g): Bare 27614, 6 (6, 6, 7, 8) hanks

NEEDLES
US 7 (4.5mm) 32" circular needles, or size to obtain gauge
US 6 (4mm) 32" and 16" circular needles, or one size smaller than size to obtain gauge

NOTIONS
Yarn Needle
Removable Stitch Markers
Stitch Holders
Crochet Hook (Size G/6)
Smooth Scrap Yarn
0.75" Buttons

GAUGE
22 sts and 28 rows = 4" in Diamond Texture pattern, blocked

For pattern support, contact amigurumikr@gmail.com

Valen

Notes:
Valen is a boxy-fit hooded vest with an allover diamond texture pattern. The back is wider than the front. A single column of purl stitches divides the fronts and back. The buttonholes are worked in the left band.

When working the charts, follow RS rows (odd numbers) from right to left, and WS rows (even numbers) from left to right.

Diamond Texture Pattern (worked flat over multiples of 4 sts plus 3)
Row 1 (RS): (P1, K1) to last st, P1.
Row 2 (WS): (K1, P1) to last st, K1.
Row 3: (K3, P1) to last 3 sts, K3.
Row 4: (P3, K1) to last 3 sts, P3.
Row 5: Rep Row 1.
Row 6: Rep Row 2.
Row 7: (K1, P1, K2) to last 3 sts, K1, P1, K1.
Row 8: (P1, K1, P2) to last 3 sts, P1, K1, P1.
Rep Rows 1-8 for pattern.

Wrap and Turn (W&T)
A tutorial for the Wrap and Turn (W&T) can be found at http://tutorials.knitpicks.com/wptutorials/short-rows-wrap-and-turn-or-wt/.

3-Needle Bind Off
A tutorial for the 3-Needle Bind Off can be found at https://tutorials.knitpicks.com/3-needle-bind-off/.

Kitchener Stitch
A tutorial for the Kitchener Stitch can be found at http://tutorials.knitpicks.com/wptutorials/kitchener-stitch/.

4-St One Row Buttonhole
WYIF, SL 1 st P-wise, WYIB, *SL 1 st P-wise, pass first slipped st over next st; rep from * 3 more times. Turn garment. Cable CO 5 sts. Turn garment, WYIB SL first st on LH needle onto RH needle and pass last CO st over it.

Mattress Stitch
Lay out your pieces next to each other, RS facing up, bottom edges toward you. Thread the tail of yarn on a yarn needle. Bring your needle under the thread; then PU the running thread between the first and second sts on the opposing piece. Work back and forth from running thread to running thread to running thread, keeping the tension easy but firm.

DIRECTIONS
Body
Hem
CO 229 (245, 261, 277, 293) sts with smaller needle.
Rib Band Setup Row (WS): SSP, (K1, P1) to last 3 sts, K1, P2tog. 227 (243, 259, 275, 291) sts.
Rib Band Row 1 (RS): (K1, P1) to last st, K1.
Rib Band Row 2 (WS): (P1, K1) to last st, P1.
Rib Band Row 3: (K1, P1) to last 9 sts, work 4-St One Row Buttonhole, (P1, K1) to end.
Rep Rib Band Rows 2 and 1 two times.
Rep Rib Band Row 2 once more.
Rep Rib Band Rows 3 and 2 once more.
End with WS.

Setup Row 1 (RS): (K1, P1) 5 times. Place just worked 10 sts on stitch holder. Switch to larger needle, M1R, (K1, P1, K2) 9 (10, 11, 12, 13) times, K1, P1, K1, PM for side seam, P1, PM, (K1, P1, K2) 31 (33, 35, 37, 39) times, K1, P1, K1, PM for side seam, P1, PM, (K1, P1, K2) 9 (10, 11, 12, 13) times, K1, P1, K1, M1L. Place next 10 sts on stitch holder or scrap yarn. 209 (225, 241, 257, 273) sts.
Work Setup Row 2 on Valen Stitch Chart. 40 (44, 48, 52, 56) sts for each Front, a single P st for each side seam, 127 (135, 143, 151, 159) sts for Back. 209 (225, 241, 257, 273) total sts.

Working flat, rep Rows 1-8 of Valen Stitch Chart until piece measure 7.5" from CO edge, place removable M at the side seam st for optional Side Band.
Cont in pattern for 1.25" further from first removable M, place removable M at the next side seam for optional Side Band.
Cont in pattern until piece measures 15" from CO edge, ending with a WS row.

Divide Fronts and Back
Next Row (RS): Cont in pattern 36 (39, 42, 45, 48) sts, BO 29 (31, 33, 35, 37) sts, cont in pattern 79 (85, 91, 97, 103) sts, BO 29 (31, 33, 35, 37) sts, cont in pattern to end of row. Place removable M on the 15 (16, 17, 18, 19)th st on each BO edge. Turn garment to work Left Front.

Left Front
Next Row (WS): Cont in pattern to end of row.
Row 1 (Dec Row): SSK, cont in pattern to end of row.
Rep Dec Row every other row another 3 (4, 5, 6, 7) times. 32 (34, 36, 38, 40) sts.
Cont in pattern until piece measures 8.25 (9, 9.75, 10.5, 11.25)" from BO edge. Ending after a WS row.
Short Row 1 (RS): Cont in pattern.
Short Row 2 (WS): Cont in pattern to last 4 (4, 4, 5, 5) sts, W&T.
Short Row 3: Cont in pattern.
Short Row 4: Cont in pattern 6 (7, 8, 7, 8) sts before wrapped st, W&T.
Short Row 5: Cont in pattern to end of row.
Short Row 6: (Cont in pattern to wrapped st, work wrap tog with wrapped st) twice, cont in pattern to end of row. Break yarn. Place remaining sts on stitch holder or scrap yarn.

Back
Join new yarn on WS.
Next Row (WS): Cont in pattern to end of row.
Row 1 (Dec Row, RS): SSK, cont in pattern to last 2 sts, K2tog. 2 sts dec.

Rep Dec Row every RS row another 3 (4, 5, 6, 7) times. 71 (75, 79, 83, 87) sts.
Cont in pattern until piece measures 8.25 (9, 9.75, 10.5, 11.25)" from BO edge, ending with a WS row.
Short Row 1 (RS): Cont in pattern to last 4 (4, 4, 5, 5) sts, W&T.
Short Row 2 (WS): Cont in pattern to last 4 (4, 4, 5, 5) sts, W&T.
Short Row 3: Cont in pattern 6 (7, 8, 7, 8) sts before wrapped st, W&T.
Short Row 4: Cont in pattern 6 (7, 8, 7, 8) sts before wrapped st, W&T.
Short Row 5: (Cont in pattern to wrapped st, work wrap tog with wrapped st) twice, cont in pattern to end of row.
Short Row 6: (Cont in pattern to wrapped st, work wrap tog with wrapped st) twice, cont in pattern to end of row.
Place remaining sts on stitch holder or scrap yarn. Break yarn and leave 36" yarn tail for 3-Needle Bind Off.

Right Front

Join new yarn on WS.
Next Row (WS): Cont in pattern to end of row.
Row 1 (Dec Row, RS): Cont in pattern to last 2 sts, K2tog.
Rep Dec Row every other row another 3 (4, 5, 6, 7) times. 32 (34, 36, 38, 40) sts.
Cont in pattern until piece measures 8.25 (9, 9.75, 10.5, 11.25)" from BO edge. ending with a WS row.
Short Row 1 (RS): Cont in pattern to last 4 (4, 4, 5, 5) sts, W&T.
Short Row 2 (WS): Cont in pattern.
Short Row 3: Cont in pattern 6 (7, 8, 7, 8) sts before wrapped st, W&T.
Short Row 4: Cont in pattern.
Short Row 5: (Cont in pattern to wrapped st, work wrap tog with wrapped st) twice, cont in pattern to end.
Short Row 6: Cont in pattern. Do not break yarn; It will be used for the Hood.

Joining Shoulder

Replace remaining sts of back and left shoulder to needles. Arrange each shoulder with their the WS facing out, work a 3-Needle BO over first 15 (16, 17, 18, 19) sts, remove next 17 (18, 19, 20, 21) sts of left front piece to spare needle, BO 41 (43, 45, 47, 49) sts on center back only, remove first 17 (18, 19, 20, 21) sts of right front to spare needle, 3-Needle Bind Off remaining 15 (16, 17, 18, 19) sts using remaining yarn tail on the back.

Hood

Cont in pattern over the 17 (18, 19, 20, 21) sts on right front piece, PU and K 69 (67, 65, 63, 61) sts on WS, cont in pattern over the 17 (18, 19, 20, 21) sts on left front. When picking up sts, insert the needle tip from WS to RS so the PU seam will be on the RS. 103 sts.

Next Row (WS): Cont in pattern 17 (18, 19, 20, 21) sts, P2tog, P31 (30, 20, 28, 27), PM, P3, PM, P31 (30, 20, 28, 27), SSP, cont in pattern to end. 101 sts.
Cont in pattern 6.5" from PU edge, ending with a WS row.
Next Row (Dec Row, RS): Cont in pattern 2 sts before M, K2tog, SM, then cont in pattern 3 sts, SM, SSK, cont in pattern to end. 2 sts dec. Please follow Hood Dec Guide Chart for decrease sts.
Rep Dec Row every RS row 19 more times, end with RS. 61 sts. Remove Markers.
Turn garment WS facing, then work a 3-Needle Bind Off.

Sleeve Band (make 2 the same)

Using smooth scrap yarn and crochet hook, chain 10 sts. PU 10 sts on back loops of chains using smaller knitting needle and working yarn.
Row 1 (RS): K2, (P1, K1) 4 times.
Row 2 (WS): P2, (K1, P1) 4 times.

Valen 85

Rep Rows 1–2 until piece measures 8.5 (9.25, 10.25, 10.75, 11)" from CO edge, PM, cont in pattern another 8.5 (9.25, 10.25, 10.75, 11)", ending with a WS row. Total length is 17 (18.5, 20.5, 21.5, 22)".

Undo crochet chains and transfer remaining 10 sts to spare needle. Being careful to not twist the band, graft (Kitchener St) the K sts only on the RS. Turn the band and graft remaining K sts together.

Right Front Band

Place previously held 10 sts on smaller needle, join new yarn on WS, (P1, K1) 5 times on WS.
(P1, K1) 5 times on RS.
Rep last 2 rows until band measures 36.25 (37, 37.75, 38.5, 39.25)" from CO edge, ending with a WS row.

Left Front Band

Place previously held 10 sts on smaller needle, join new yarn on RS.
(P1, K1) 5 times on RS, (P1, K1) 5 times on WS.
Rep last 2 rows until band measures 36.25 (37, 37.75, 38.5, 39.25)" from CO edge, ending with a WS row and AT THE SAME TIME make 4 One Row Buttonholes every 3". Total 6 buttonholes on the band.

Being careful to not twist the band, graft (Kitchener St) the K sts only on the RS. Turn the band and graft remaining K sts together.

Side Band (make 2 the same, optional)

Front side up and RS facing, PU and K 11 sts between the 2 Ms on the edge of back.
Next Row (WS): (P1, K1) 5 times, P1.
Next Row (RS): (K1, P1) 5 times, K1.
Rep last 2 rows until band measures 4.25" from PU edge, while at the same time making 2 One Row Buttonholes, the first when band measures 3.25" from PU, and the second at 4" from PU, ending with a WS row. BO all sts.

Finishing

Remove markers. Sew Body Band to body using Mattress st. Sew on Sleeve Bands, matching M to shoulder seams. Weave in ends, wash and block to schematic measurements. When fully dry, sew on buttons.

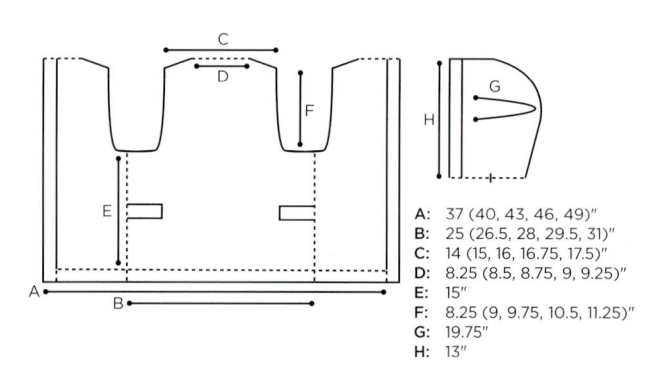

A: 37 (40, 43, 46, 49)"
B: 25 (26.5, 28, 29.5, 31)"
C: 14 (15, 16, 16.75, 17.5)"
D: 8.25 (8.5, 8.75, 9, 9.25)"
E: 15"
F: 8.25 (9, 9.75, 10.5, 11.25)"
G: 19.75"
H: 13"

86 Valen

Legend:

☐ **Knit**
RS: knit stitch
WS: purl stitch

• **Purl**
RS: purl stitch
WS: knit stitch

\ **SSK**
Slip one stitch as if to knit, slip another stitch as if to knit. Insert left-hand needle into front of these 2 stitches and knit them together

\ **SSP**
Slip one stitch as if to purl, slip another stitch as if to purl. Slip these stitches back to the left-hand needle and purl stitches together through the back loop

/ **K2tog**
Knit two stitches together as one stitch

/ **P2tog**
Purl two stitches together as one stitch

☐ **Pattern Repeat**

| **Marker**

Diamond Texture Pattern Chart

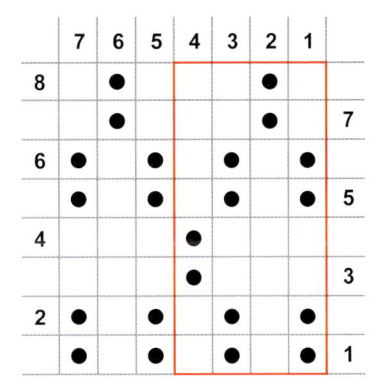

Hood Dec Guide Chart

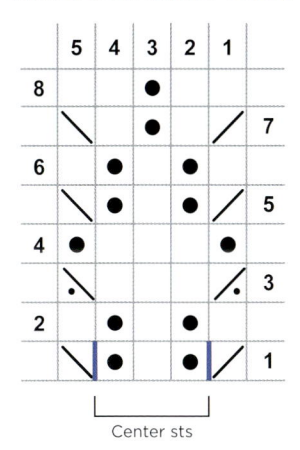

Center sts

Valen Stitch Chart

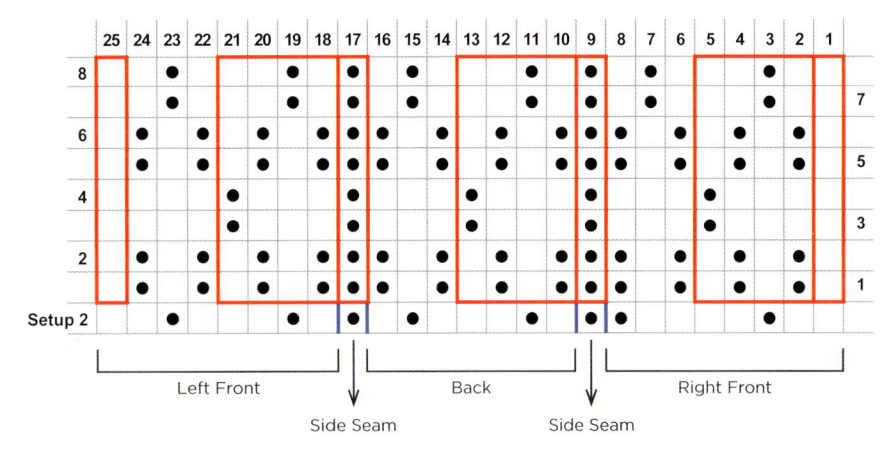

Left Front — Side Seam — Back — Side Seam — Right Front

Valen 87

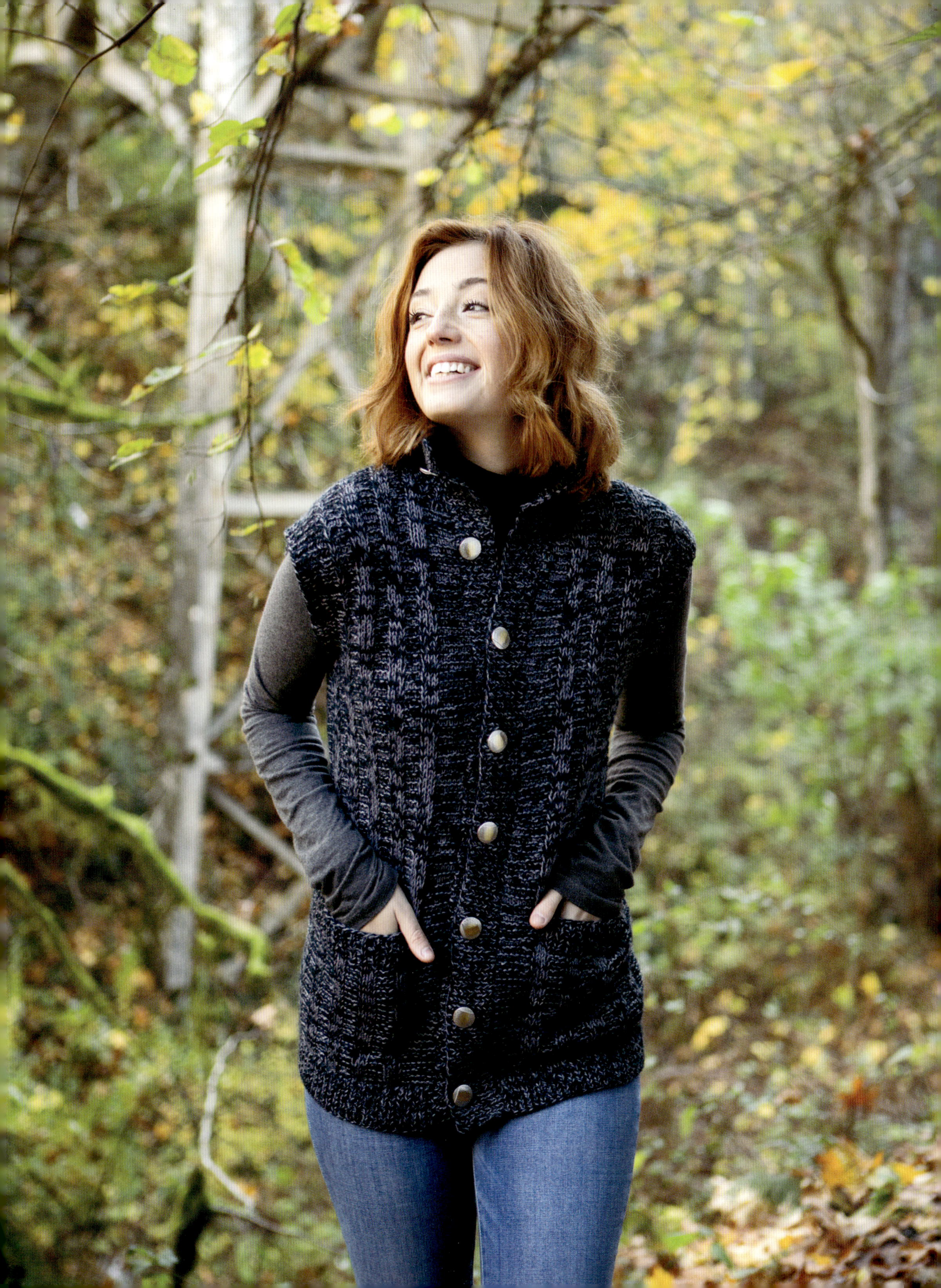

WAYFARER VEST

by Stacey Gerbman

FINISHED MEASUREMENTS
38.5 (41.5, 44.5, 47.25, 49.75, 53.5)" finished bust measurement, buttoned; garment is meant to be worn with 2-4" of positive ease

YARN
Knit Picks Wool of the Andes (sport weight, 100% Peruvian Highland Wool; 137 yards/50g): 25661 Midnight Heather, 7 (8, 9, 10, 10, 11) skeins
Knit Picks Palette (fingering weight, 100% Peruvian Highland Wool; 231 yards/50g): 24244 Marble Heather, 4 (4, 5, 5, 6, 6) skeins

NEEDLES
US 6 (4mm) 16, 32, and 40" circular needles, or size to obtain gauge
US 8 (5mm) 16, 32, and 40" circular needles, or size to obtain gauge

NOTIONS
Yarn Needle
Stitch Markers
Scrap Yarn or Stitch Holder
(8) 1.25-1.5" Buttons

GAUGE
17 sts and 28 rows = 4" in Garter Rib pattern holding one strand of Wool of the Andes and one strand of Palette tog on larger needles, blocked
23 sts and 28 rows = 4" in K1, P1 Rib holding one strand of Wool of the Andres and one strand of Palette tog on smaller needles, blocked

For pattern support, contact staceygerbman@gmail.com

Wayfarer Vest

Notes:
Pattern is worked holding one strand of Wool of the Andes and one of Palette together.

The pocket linings are knit first, and then the body of this vest is knit flat to the joining of the linings and then up to the armholes. The two front sections and the back are worked separately to the shoulder. Stitches at the neck are picked up to knit the high collar. Stitches for the front bands are picked up and knit back and forth. Finally, stitches are picked up around the armholes and knit in 1x1 Rib for a clean edge finish.

Use different colored markers to indicate side seams.

Garter Stitch (worked flat over any number of sts)
All Rows: Knit.

1x1 Rib (worked flat over multiples of 2 sts plus 1 st for Body, Collar, and Button bands; worked in the rnd over multiples of 2 sts for Armhole opening)
Row/Rnd 1 (RS): (K1, P1) to end for Armholes, or to last st, K1, for Body, Collar, and Button band.
Row 2 (WS): (P1, K1) to last st, P1, for Body, Collar, and Button band.
Rep Rows 1-2 for pattern. When working the Armhole in the rnd, rep Rnd 1 for all rnds.

Garter Rib (worked flat over multiples of 6 sts; 6 sts plus 3 sts when working pockets)
Row 1 (RS): Knit across.
Row 2 (WS): (P3, K3) to end.
Rep Rows 1-2 for pattern.

Sloped Bind Off
Step 1: Work the first BO rows at the garment edges as usual.
Step 2: One row before the next BO row, work to the last st of the row, turn.
Step 3: Slip the first st from the LH needle P-wise, pass the unworked st of the previous row over the slipped st (the first st is bound off). BO remaining sts as usual.
Rep Steps 2-3 for remaining BO rows.

Backward Loop CO
*Use the working yarn to make a loop around your left thumb, then place this loop onto the RH needle; rep from * until you have the required number of sts on your needle.

DIRECTIONS

Pocket Linings (make 2 the same)
CO 27 sts with larger 16" circular needle. Work flat in St st (K on RS, P on WS) for 6". Place sts on holder.

Body
With smaller needle CO 209 (225, 243, 261, 273, 295) sts using 32" or 40" circular needle.
Work 1x1 Rib for 2", ending with a RS row. Switch to larger needle.

Decrease Row (WS): P all sts decreasing 54 (58, 62, 68, 70, 76) sts evenly across row. 155 (167, 181, 193, 203, 219) sts.

Torso
Setup Row (RS): K4 (1, 5, 2, 4, 0), PM(1), work Row 1 of Garter Rib pattern over next 30 (36, 36, 42, 42, 48) sts, PM(2), K3, PM(3) to indicate side seam, work Row 1 of Garter Rib pattern over next 78 (84, 90, 96, 102, 114) sts, PM(4), K3, PM(5) to indicate side seam, work Row 1 of Garter Rib pattern over next 30 (36, 36, 42, 42, 48) sts, PM(6), K7 (4, 8, 5, 7, 3) to end.

Work across sts, following Garter Rib pattern as set between M 1 and 2, M 3 and 4, and M 5 and 6. Work all other sts in Garter st. End with a WS row when piece measures 8" from CO edge.

Pocket Placement
K5 (7, 9, 10, 11, 12), place next 27 sts on a holder, with RS of pocket lining facing you K 27 sts over pocket lining, work across to last 34 (34, 36, 37, 38, 39) sts, place the next 27 sts on a holder, with RS of pocket lining facing you K 27 sts over pocket lining, K7 (7, 9, 10, 11, 12).

Work sweater maintaining Garter Rib pattern between set markers until piece measures 16.5 (17, 17.25, 17.25, 17.25, 17.25)" from CO edge or desired length to underarm, ending with a WS row.

Divide for Fronts and Back
K 37 (40, 44, 47, 49, 51) sts for right front, transfer next 81 (87, 93, 99, 105, 117) sts to stitch holder or scrap yarn for back, then transfer last 37 (40, 44, 47, 49, 51) sts to separate stitch holder or scrap yarn for left front.

Right Front
Please read the following section through to the end. Review Sloped Bind Off technique.
Shape Armhole
BO 4 (4, 4, 4, 4, 5) sts at the beginning of the next WS row, then BO 3 (3, 4, 4, 4, 4) sts at the beginning of the following WS row, then BO 2 (3, 3, 3, 4, 4) sts at the beginning of following WS row, then BO 1 (3, 3, 3, 3, 3) sts at the beginning of the following WS row, then BO 0 (0, 0, 0, 0, 2) sts of the following WS row.

Upon completion of armhole shaping, you will have 10 (13, 14, 14, 15, 18) sts fewer at armhole edge.

Right Front Neck Shaping
Continue working straight in pattern until piece measures 6.75 (6.75, 7.25, 7.75, 8.25, 8.75)" from beginning of armhole shaping ending with a WS row, then shape neck as follows:
Neck Decrease Row (RS): BO 3 sts, work as established to end, then BO 2 (2, 2, 3, 2, 2) sts at the beginning of the following RS row, then BO 1 (1, 2, 2, 2, 1) sts at the beginning of the next 3 RS rows, then BO 1 st at the beginning of the following 4 RS rows. 12 (12, 15, 16, 15, 12) sts decreased at neck edge.

AT THE SAME TIME Shape Right Shoulder
Use the Sloped Bind Off in this section for best results. When armhole measures 8.5 (8.5, 9, 9.5, 10, 10.5)", BO 5 (5, 5, 7, 7, 7) sts at the beginning of the next WS row, then BO 5 (5, 5, 5, 7, 7) sts at the beginning of the following WS row and then BO remaining 5 (5, 5, 5, 5, 7) sts at the beginning of the following WS row.

Back
Transfer held 81 (87, 93, 99, 105, 117) back sts to needle and rejoin yarn ready to work a RS row.
Shape Armholes
Use the Sloped Bind Off in this section for best results. BO 4 (4, 4, 4, 4, 5) sts at the beginning of the next 2 rows, then BO 3 (3, 4, 4, 4, 4) sts at the beginning of the following 2 rows, then BO 2 (3, 3, 3, 4, 4) sts at the beginning of following 2 rows, then BO 1 (3, 3, 3, 3, 3) sts at the beginning of the following 2 rows, then BO 0 (0, 0, 0, 0, 2) sts of the following 2 rows. 61 (61, 65, 71, 75, 81) sts.

Continue working straight in pattern until piece measures 8.5 (8.5, 9, 9.5, 10, 10.5)" from beginning of armhole shaping ending with a WS row.

Shape Shoulders
Use the Sloped Bind Off in this section for best results.
BO 5 (5, 5, 7, 7, 7) sts at the beginning of the next 2 rows, then BO 5 (5, 5, 5, 7, 7) sts at the beginning of the following 2 rows and then BO 5 (5, 5, 5, 5, 7) sts at the beginning of the following 2 rows.
Transfer remaining 31 (31, 35, 37, 37, 39) sts to stitch holder or scrap yarn for back neck.

Left Front
Please read the following section through to the end.
Review Sloped Bind Off technique.
Shape Armhole
BO 4 (4, 4, 4, 4, 5) sts at the beginning of the next RS row, then BO 3 (3, 4, 4, 4, 4) sts at the beginning of the following RS row, then BO 2 (3, 3, 3, 4, 4) sts at the beginning of following RS row, then BO 1 (3, 3, 3, 3, 3) sts at the beginning of the following RS row, then BO 0 (0, 0, 0, 0, 2) sts of the following RS row. Upon completion of armhole shaping, you will have 10 (13, 14, 14, 15, 18) sts fewer at armhole edge.

Left Front Neck Shaping
Continue working straight in pattern until piece measures 6.75 (6.75, 7.25, 7.75, 8.25, 8.75)" from beginning of armhole shaping ending with a RS row, then shape neck as follows:
Neck Decrease Row (WS): BO 3 sts, work as established to end, then BO 2 (2, 2, 3, 2, 2) sts at the beginning of the following WS row, then BO 1 (1, 2, 2, 2, 1) sts at the beginning of the next 3 WS rows, then BO 1 st at the beginning of the following 4 WS rows. 12 (12, 15, 16, 15, 12) sts decreased at neck edge.

AT THE SAME TIME Shape Left Shoulder
Use the sloped Bind Off in this section for best results.
When armhole measures 8.5 (8.5, 9, 9.5, 10, 10.5)", BO 5 (5, 5, 7, 7, 7) sts at the beginning of the next RS row, then BO 5 (5, 5, 5, 7, 7) sts at the beginning of the following RS row and then BO remaining 5 (5, 5, 5, 5, 7) sts at the beginning of the following RS row.

Finishing
Sew the sides of the pocket linings to inside of the sweater (not the bottoms yet).
PU and K27 pocket sts using larger needle and work 1x1 Rib for 1.5".
BO loosely and sew down edges to sweater front.
Rep with second pocket.

Sew Shoulder Seams.
Weave in ends, wash and block to diagram.
Sew bottoms of pocket linings to inside of sweater.

Neck
With smaller circular needle, beginning at right front neck edge, PU and K 12 (12, 15, 16, 15, 12) sts of right front neck, then PU and K 31 (31, 35, 37, 37, 39) held back neck sts, then PU and K 12 (12, 15, 16, 15, 12) sts from left neck edge. Total of 55 (55, 65, 69, 67, 63) sts.
Work flat in 1x1 Rib for 4".
BO loosely.

Wayfarer Vest

Right and Left Armholes
With smaller needle and RS facing PU and K 98 (98, 104, 110, 114, 122) sts, PM for beginning of the rnd.
Work 1x1 Rib in the rnd for 2".
BO all sts.

Button Bands
Right Front Button Band
With smaller circular needle, beginning at bottom right front PU and K 157 (161, 163, 167, 169, 173) sts along right front and neck edge.
Work 1x1 Rib for 2".
BO all sts.

Left Front Button Band
With smaller circular needle beginning at top left front neck edge PU and K 157 (161, 163, 167, 169, 173) sts along left front neck and body edge.
Work in 1x1 Rib for 1" ending with a WS row.
Buttonhole Row: (K1, P1) for 8 sts, BO 2 sts, * (K1, P1) for 18 (18, 18, 19, 19, 20) sts, BO 2 sts; rep from * 7 times, (K1, P1) for remaining 7 (11, 13, 10, 12, 9) sts.
Next Row: Work (P1, K1) for 7 (11, 13, 10, 12, 9) sts, CO 2 sts using Backward Loop Cast On method, *(P1, K1) for 18 (18, 18, 19, 19, 20) sts, CO 2 sts; rep from * 7 times, (P1, K2) for remaining 8 sts.
Continue working in 1x1 Rib until band measures 2" from pick up edge.
BO all sts.

Weave in any remaining ends invisibly on the WS of fabric.
Gently wet-block entire garment.
Attach buttons opposite buttonholes when dry.

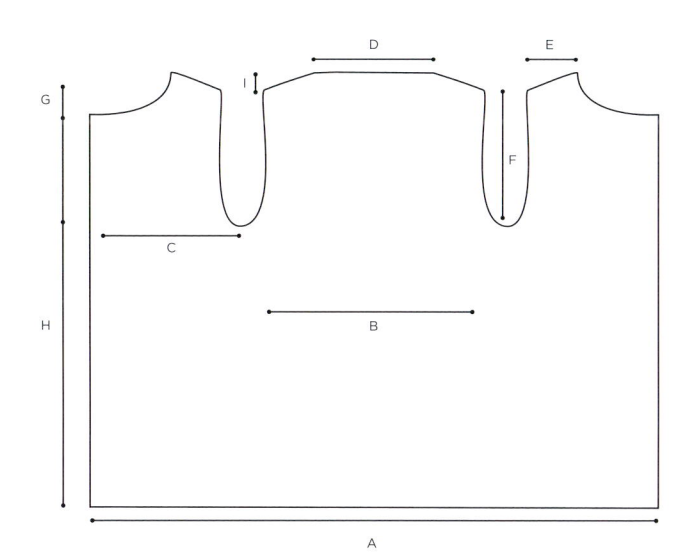

Finished Bust Measurement: 38.5 (41.5, 44.5, 47.25, 49.75, 53.5)"
A: 36.5 (39.5, 42.5, 45.25, 47.75, 51.5)"
B: 19 (20.5, 22, 23.25, 24.75, 27.5)"
C: 8.75 (9.5, 10.25, 11, 11.5, 12)"
D: 7.25 (7.25, 8.25, 8.75, 8.75, 9.25)"
E: 3.5 (3.5, 3.5, 4, 4.5, 5)"
F: 8.5 (8.5, 9, 9.5, 10, 10.5)"
G: 2.75"

Wayfarer Vest

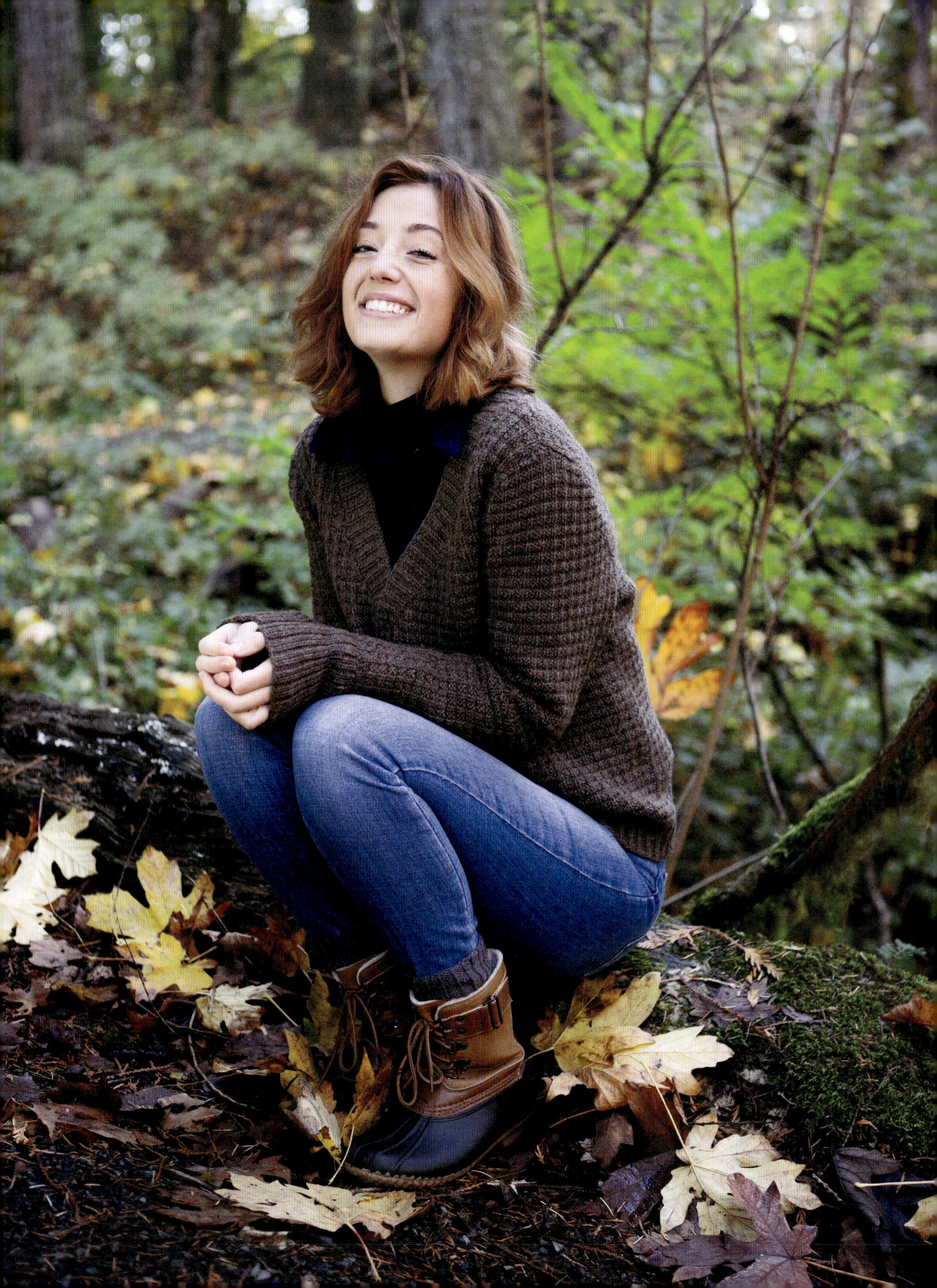

WEMBLEY SWEATER

by Cassie Castillo

FINISHED MEASUREMENTS
35.5 (39.75, 43.75, 48, 52.25, 56.25, 60.5)" finished bust measurement; garment is meant to be worn with 4" ease

YARN
Knit Picks Simply Wool (worsted weight, 100% Eco Wool; 218 yards/100g): Wallace 27472, 7 (8, 8, 9, 9, 10, 11) hanks

NEEDLES
US 7 (4.5-mm) 32" circular needles and DPNs, or size to obtain gauge

US 6 (4-mm) 32" circular needles and DPNs, or one size smaller than size to obtain gauge

NOTIONS
Yarn Needle
Stitch Markers
Scrap Yarn or Stitch Holders

GAUGE
23 sts and 32 rnds = 4" in Waffle Stitch on larger needles in the rnd, blocked

For pattern support, contact cassiemiller820@yahoo.com

Wembley Sweater

Notes:
A highly textured waffle stitch pattern is paired with a classic silhouette in the Wembley Sweater. Worked from the bottom up, the body and sleeves are worked separately in the round. A 1x2 rib flows seamlessly into the easy-to-knit waffle stitch. Turn back cuffs and an overlapping V-neck band add sophisticated details to an otherwise simple sweater.

Incorporate new stitches into stitch pattern: when working neck and armhole decreases, keep a 1-stitch stockinette stitch selvage for easy sewing later on.

Waffle Stitch (in the rnd over multiples of 3 sts)
Rnds 1-2: (K1, P2) to end.
Rnds 3-4: K all.
Rep Rnds 1-4 for pattern.

Waffle Stitch (worked flat over multiples of 3 sts)
Row 1 (RS): (K1, P2) to end.
Row 2 (WS): (K2, P1) to end.
Row 3: K across.
Row 4: P across.
Rep Rows 1-4 for pattern.

1x2 Rib (in the rnd over multiples of 3 sts)
All rnds: (K1, P2) to end.

1x2 Rib (worked flat over multiples of 3 sts)
Row 1 (RS): (K1, P2) to end.
Row 2: (K2, P1) to end.
Reps Rows 1-2 for pattern.

Reverse Rib (in the round over multiples of 3 sts)
All Rnds: (P1, K2) to end.

DIRECTIONS

Body
With smaller circular needles, loosely CO 204 (228, 252, 276, 300, 324, 348) sts. PM and join in the rnd, being careful not to twist sts.
Work in 1x2 Rib until piece measures 2" from CO edge. Change to larger needles. Work in Waffle St until piece measures 14.75 (15, 15.25, 15.5, 15.75, 16, 15.5)", ending with an odd-numbered rnd.

Next Rnd, Marker Setup: Work 102 (114, 126, 138, 150, 162, 174) sts, PM for armhole, work in pattern to end.

Divide Neck
Cut yarn. SL M and next 46 (52, 58, 64, 70, 76, 79) sts to RH needle and rejoin yarn. BO 10 sts for neck, work to end. Body will now be worked flat in rows, beginning and ending with neck edges. Armhole shaping begins before neck shaping ends. Read through following section before continuing. 194 (218, 242, 266, 290, 314, 338) sts.

Next Row (WS): P1, work to last st, P1.

Neck Dec Row (RS): SSK, work to last 2 sts, K2tog. 2 sts dec.
Rep Neck Dec Row every RS row 14 (13, 14, 15, 14, 15, 17) more times, then every 4th row 9 (10, 10, 10, 11, 11, 12) times.
AT THE SAME TIME, when piece measures 16", on a RS row, divide front and back.

Divide Body (RS): *Work to 4 (6, 7, 9, 10, 12, 13) sts before M, BO 8 (12, 14, 18, 20, 24, 26) sts; rep from * one more time, work to end.

Next Row (WS): Work Left Front to armhole BO, place 94 (102, 112, 120, 130, 138, 148) Back sts onto holder, join another ball of yarn to Right Front and work to end. Both Fronts will be worked at the same time. While continuing neck shaping, begin armhole shaping.

Front
Armhole Dec Row (RS): Work to last 2 sts of Right Front, K2tog, move to Left Front, SSK, work to end. 1 st dec each front.
Rep Armhole Dec Row every RS row 5 (6, 9, 10, 12, 13, 15) more times. When all shaping is complete, 12 (15, 16, 18, 21, 23, 23) sts.

Cont in pattern until armhole measures 8 (8.5, 9, 9.5, 10, 10.5, 11)", ending with a WS row.

Shape Shoulder (RS): Work across Right Front, BO 4 (5, 5, 6, 7, 8, 7) sts on Left Front, work to end.
Shape Shoulder (WS): Work across Left Front, BO 4 (5, 5, 6, 7, 8, 7) sts on Right Front, work to end.
Rep last 2 rows one more time. BO all sts.

Back
Place held 94 (102, 112, 120, 130, 138, 148) sts onto needle with WS facing. Work in pattern.
Armhole Dec Row (RS): SSK, work to last 2 sts, K2tog. 2 sts dec.
Rep Armhole Dec Row every RS row 5 (6, 9, 10, 12, 13, 15) more times. 82 (88, 92, 98, 104, 110, 116) sts.

Cont in pattern until armhole measures 8 (8.5, 9, 9.5, 10, 10.5, 11)", ending with a WS row. BO 4 (5, 5, 6, 7, 8, 7) sts at the beginning of the next 4 rows. 66 (68, 72, 74, 76, 78, 88) sts. BO all sts.

Sleeves (make 2 the same)
With smaller DPNs, loosely CO 48 (48, 54, 60, 66, 66, 72) sts. PM and join in the rnd, being careful not to twist sts.
Work in Reverse Rib until piece measures 5" from CO edge. Change to larger DPNs.
Next Rnd: M1L, work in Waffle St to end. 49 (49, 55, 61, 67, 67, 73) sts.
Next Rnd: K1, work in Waffle St to end.
Inc Rnd: K1, M1L, work in pattern to last st, M1R. 2 sts inc.
Rep Inc Rnd every 8 (6, 6, 6, 6, 6, 4)th rnd 4 (3, 3, 3, 7, 18, 4) more times, then every 10 (8, 8, 8, 8, 0, 6)th rnd 7 (11, 11, 11, 8, 0, 14) times. 73 (79, 85, 91, 99, 105, 111) sts.

Cont in pattern until piece measures 19.75 (20, 20, 20, 20, 20.25, 21)" ending with an even-numbered rnd and stopping 4 (6, 7, 9, 10, 12, 13) sts before M.
Divide Sleeve: BO 8 (12, 14, 18, 20, 24, 26) sts, work to end. Sleeve cap will now be worked flat in rows. 65 (67, 71, 73, 79, 81, 85) sts.
Next Row (WS): P1, work in pattern to last st, P1.

Sleeve Dec Row (RS): SSK, work to last 2 sts, K2tog. 2 sts dec.
Rep Sleeve Dec Row every RS row 8 (8, 8, 7, 9, 8, 8) more times, then every 4th row 3 (3, 4, 6, 4, 6, 7) times, then every RS row 9 (10, 9, 8, 11, 9, 9) times. 23 (23, 27, 29, 29, 33, 35) sts.

BO 8 (8, 9, 10, 10, 11, 12) sts at the beginning of the next 2 rows. BO all sts.

Finishing
Weave in ends, wash, and block to diagram.
Sew shoulder seams.

Neckband
With smaller circular needles and RS facing, beginning at Right Front neck edge (not including BO edge) PU and K 58 (60, 62, 62, 65, 66, 72) sts to shoulder seam, 59 (59, 61, 63, 63, 65, 75) sts along Back neck to shoulder seam, and 58 (60, 62, 62, 65, 66, 72) sts along Left Front neck edge, ending before BO edge. 175 (179, 185, 187, 193, 197, 219) sts.

Next Row (WS): P1, *K2, P1; rep from * to end.
Next Row (RS): K1, *P2, K1; rep from * to end.
Rep last 2 rows until rib measures 1.75", ending with a WS row. BO all sts, cut yarn leaving a tail long enough to sew the rib edges.

Overlap rib edges and sew to BO edge.
Sew sleeves into armholes.
Weave in remaining ends.

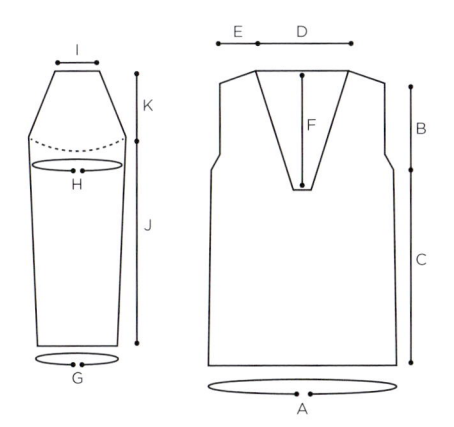

- **A:** 35.5 (39.75, 43.75, 48, 52.25, 56.25, 60.5)"
- **B:** 8 (8.5, 9, 9.5, 10, 10.5, 11)"
- **C:** 16"
- **D:** 10 (10, 10.5, 10.75, 10.75, 11.25, 13.25)"
- **E:** 2 (2.5, 2.75, 3.25, 3.75, 4, 4)"
- **F:** 9.25 (9.5, 9.75, 10, 10.25, 10.5, 11.5)"
- **G:** 8.25 (8.25, 9.5, 10.5, 11.5, 11.5, 12.5)"
- **H:** 12.75 (13.75, 14.75, 15.75, 17.25, 18.25, 19.25)"
- **I:** 4 (4, 4.75, 5, 5, 5.75, 6)"
- **J:** 19.75 (20, 20, 20, 20, 20.25, 21)"
- **K:** 6.5 (6.75, 7, 7.5, 7.75, 8, 8.5)"

Wembley Sweater

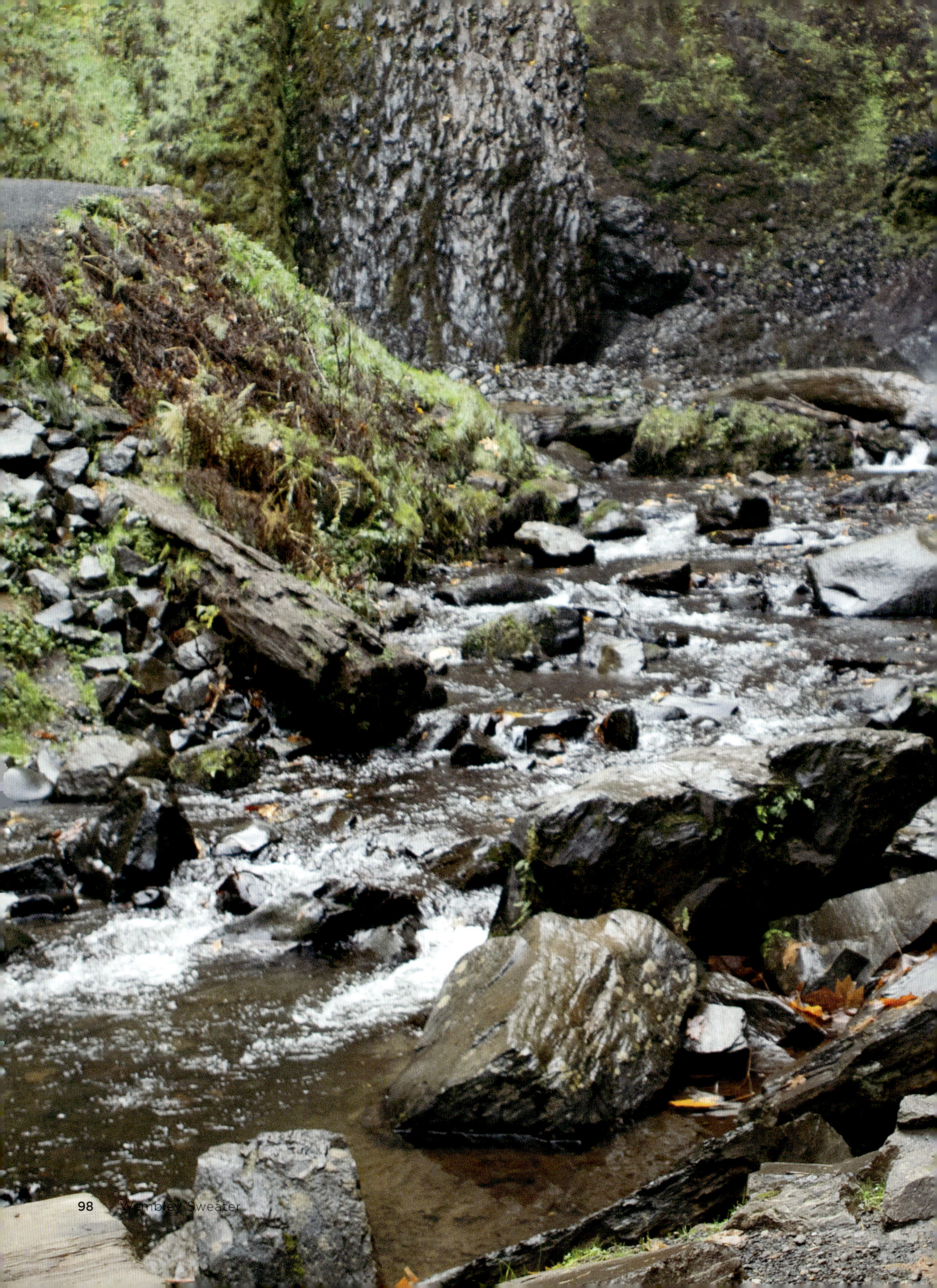

Abbreviations

BO	bind off	KFB	knit into the front and back of stitch	PU	pick up	SSP	sl, sl, p these 2 sts tog tbl
cn	cable needle			P-wise	purlwise		
CC	contrast color	K-wise	knitwise	rep	repeat	SSSK	sl, sl, sl, k these 3 sts tog
CDD	centered double dec	LH	left hand	Rev St st	reverse stockinette stitch		
		M	marker			St st	stockinette stitch
CO	cast on	M1	make one stitch	RH	right hand	sts	stitch(es)
cont	continue	M1L	make one left-leaning stitch	rnd(s)	round(s)	TBL	through back loop
dec	decrease(es)			RS	right side	TFL	through front loop
DPN(s)	double pointed needle(s)	M1R	make one right-leaning stitch	Sk	skip	tog	together
				Sk2p	sl 1, k2tog, pass slipped stitch over k2tog: 2 sts dec	W&T	wrap & turn (see specific instructions in pattern)
EOR	every other row	MC	main color				
inc	increase	P	purl				
K	knit	P2tog	purl 2 sts together	SKP	sl, k, psso: 1 st dec	WE	work even
K2tog	knit two sts together	PM	place marker	SL	slip	WS	wrong side
		PFB	purl into the front and back of stitch	SM	slip marker	WYIB	with yarn in back
K3tog	knit three sts together			SSK	sl, sl, k these 2 sts tog	WYIF	with yarn in front
		PSSO	pass slipped stitch over			YO	yarn over

100

Knit Picks

Knit Picks yarn is both luxe and affordable—a seeming contradiction trounced! But it's not just about the pretty colors; we also care deeply about fiber quality and fair labor practices, leaving you with a gorgeously reliable product you'll turn to time and time again.

THIS COLLECTION FEATURES

Hawthorne Tonal Hand Paint
Fingering Weight
80% Superwash Fine Highland Wool, 20% Polyamide (Nylon)

Palette
Fingering Weight
100% Peruvian Highland Wool

Provincial Tweed
Worsted Weight
80% Superwash Fine Highland Wool, 20% Donegal

Swish
DK & Worsted Weights
100% Fine Superwash Merino Wool

Simply Wool
Worsted & Bulky Weights
100% Eco Wool

Stroll
Fingering Weight
75% Fine Superwash Merino Wool, 25% Nylon

Stroll Tweed
Fingering Weight
65% Fine Superwash Merino Wool, 25% Nylon, 10% Donegal

Woodland Tweed
Aran Weight
80% Merino Wool, 15% Baby Alpaca, 5% Viscose

Wool of the Andes
Sport & Worsted Weights
100% Peruvian Highland Wool

Wool of the Andes Tweed
Worsted Weight
80% Peruvian Highland Wool, 20% Donegal

View these beautiful yarns and more at www.KnitPicks.com